Essential
Food & Drink
Italy

by Susan Conte

Susan Conte studied domestic science
and taught cookery before marrying her
Italian husband. She has lived and travelled
extensively in Italy for over 2 years and has
a broad knowledge of and great enthusiasm
for Italian cuisine. She is author of a book
on authentic pasta and pizzas.

Above: neatly stacked vines in the flourishing wine

AA Publishing

*Local markets are the best
place to buy fresh produce
Front cover: a typical
Venetian restaurant;
Annunziata Barcio wine;
traditional pasta dish
Back cover: oyster
mushrooms*

Written by Susan Conte

Edited, designed and produced by AA Publishing.
© Automobile Association Developments Limited 2001
Maps © Automobile Association Developments
Limited 2001
Reprinted Sep 2001
Reprinted Jan 2006
Reprinted Apr 2006
Reprinted May 2007

A CIP catalogue record for this book is available from the
British Library.

    The contents of this publication are believed correct at
the time of printing. Nevertheless, the publishers cannot
be held responsible for any errors or omissions or for
changes in the details given in this guide or for the
consequences of any reliance on the information provided
by the same. This does not affect your statutory rights.
Assessments are based upon the author's own experience
and, therefore, descriptions given in this guide necessarily
contain an element of subjective opinion which may not
reflect the publisher's opinion or dictate a reader's own
experience on another occasion.

    We have tried to ensure accuracy in this guide, but
things do change and we would be grateful if readers
would advise us of any inaccuracies they may encounter.

Published by AA Publishing, a trading name of Automobile
Association Developments Limited, whose registered
office is Fanum House, Basing View, Basingstoke,
Hampshire, RG21 4EA.
Registered number 1878835.

Colour separation: Chroma Graphics (Overseas) Pte Ltd,
Singapore
Printed and bound in Italy by Printer Trento srl

A03372

Find out more about
AA Publishing and the
wide range of services
the AA provides by
visiting our web site at
www.theAA.com/travel

Contents

About this Book

One of the pleasures of travelling is sampling the local food and drink. Whether your tastes are adventurous or conservative, this book will whet your appetite and give you a genuine taste of Italy. It is the perfect companion to any meal, and may even change your ideas about what's on offer – it's not all pizza and pasta! Not only will it help you to appreciate the true flavours of the country, it will enable you to cope with new or unfamiliar situations, taking the worry out of getting what you want. This book is organised into the following sections:

FOOD OF ITALY

Italy's regions are colourfully described, with the emphasis on local foods and specialities, and a look at the influences and traditions that you can still detect in them.

A comprehensive A–Z covers the foods you are likely to see in shops and markets and the dishes that appear on menus, with star ratings to help you make choices. Where items in this list are mentioned elsewhere in the text they are printed in small capitals, thus: GNOCCHI.

WINE AND DRINK OF ITALY

There is information and advice on wines and an A–Z of other drinks, both alcoholic and non-alcoholic, also star rated.

EATING OUT

The Eating Out section can help you decide where to eat and at what time. There are also tips on catering for babies and children, and special diets.

EATING IN

The guide to shopping describes the different types of establishments and what services they offer, what you can buy and when it is in season. The recipes, using typical Italian ingredients, include some of the most famous regional dishes and will appeal to cooks of all abilities.

PRACTICAL INFORMATION

This is a highly visual section containing essential information like coping with a tight budget, planning a self-catering holiday and understanding the local currency. A short section highlights the types of food and dishes eaten on high days and holidays.

Understanding the menu can sometimes be a problem and the language section gives useful words and phrases to use in a variety of establishments. Finally, there is a conversion table to help with shopping.

Grocery barge, Venice

Food of
Italy

Above: *inventive Italian pasta*
Right: *fruiit stall vendor*

Food of Italy

Unless you have visited Italy or been fortunate enough to find a good Italian restaurant where you live, Italian food may mean no more to you than spaghetti, tomato sauce, pizza and ice-cream. The dishes you will meet on an Italian trip, or in the pages of this guidebook, however, will hopefully, arouse your enthusiasm for this varied, adaptable and deliciously colourful Mediterranean cuisine.

There is plenty for all tastes. Starters range from the rustic freshly sliced Parma ham served on hot crunchy garlic bread to the more sophisticated chilled seafood salad packed with prawns, clams, mussels, octopus and squid. The pasta and rice combinations are never ending and you can find vegetable, fish and meat sauces to suit every occasion. Do not miss the polenta or the savoury rice risottos and, if you still have room, the excellent meat, fish and cheese dishes are waiting to tempt you. The dessert course varies from season to season with mountains of fresh fruit always available – juicy oranges, mandarins and kiwi fruit in the winter, succulent cherries, peaches, apricots and melons in the summer, not forgetting the luscious fresh figs and black and white grapes in all shapes and sizes. Mouthwatering sweets and local cheeses complete the feast.

Buon appetito!

Pizza chef creating his masterpiece

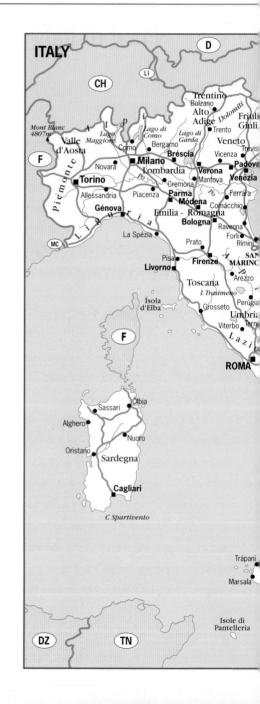

(A)

0   100   200 km
0   50   100 miles

(H)

Venezia
Udine

(SLO)

Trieste

(HR)

(YU)

Golfo di Venézia

(BIH)

Ancona

Marche
San Benedetto
Ascoli Piceno
2914m
L'Aquila ● Pescara

(YU)

Abruzzo

Molise

Latina ● Cassino   **Foggia**   Barletta
Benevento   *P u g l i a*   **Bari**

Napoli   *C a m p a n i a*

Salerno   Potenza   Brindisi
Golfo di Salerno   Lecce

Basilicata   **Táranto**

Golfo di Táranto

C a l a b r i a

Rossano

Cosenza

Crotone

Catanzaro

Isole Eólie o Lipari

Palermo   **Messina**

Réggio di Calábria
C Spartivento

Etna 3323m

Caltanissetta   **Catania**

S i c i l i a

Agrigento

Ragusa   Siracusa

C Pássero

Regions

Italy's long narrow peninsula, over 1,500km (930 miles) from top to toe, with its high mountain ranges of the Alps (Alpi), Dolomites (Dolomiti) and Apennines (Appennini), enjoys a relatively sheltered position in the middle of the Mediterranean sea.

However, the climate varies enormously from north to south and between mountain, plain and coast. This, together with a history of invasions and the fact that before the Unity of Italy in 1861 each of the individual states had its own identity, customs and cuisine, has greatly influenced Italian food. The Alpine regions are known for game and POLENTA (a type of maize porridge); the sub-Alpine parts for rice and meats; the northern valleys and plains for stuffed pastas, salami, cheeses, cream and butter: the Apennines for spicy pastoral dishes; the centre and south for olive oil and pasta; and the deep south, with its hot sun, for fruit, ripe, red tomatoes and peppers, and aubergines. Excellent fish soups and seafood around the coasts complete the picture. Common to all regions are the staples of dried beans and

Rolling Piedmontese countryside

salted cod. Whatever the dish, there is one vital element in all good Italian cooking: the use of fresh vegetables.

PIEDMONT AND VALLE D'AOSTA

The beautiful mountain region of Valle d'Aosta nestles in the shadow of Mont Blanc. The crystal-clear lakes and mountain torrents are full of trout, and many different types of game can be found in the woods and forests. The lower Alpine pastures provide succulent grazing for cattle, the grasses giving the local milk and cheese their excellent flavour. The winters, however, are very hard here, and the food must be both warming and nourishing. The first courses are mainly soups full of bread or barley, while GNOCCHI and rice served with FONTINA cheese and butter can be found all year round. FONTINA is also used to make FONDUTA ALLA VALDOSTANA, served sprinkled with slivers of truffle from neighbouring Piedmont (Piemonte). Traditionally, game, such as deer, hare and partridge, is prepared *in civet* or *in salmì* and marinated with herbs and spices for at least two days before being cooked. The salting of meat is a very old tradition, still found in certain regions; look out for the CARBONADA in the smaller *trattorie*

along the valleys. One traditional dish still easily found today is TROTA SPACCATA (spiced fried trout).

To finish the meal, especially when it is snowing outside, why not try a CAFFÈ VALDOSTANO (Valle d'Aosta-style coffee)?

Piedmont, to the south of Valle d'Aosta, gets excellent olive oil from Liguria to make one of its most traditional dishes, the savoury dip known as BAGNA CALDA. Contrasting with this simple concoction are the dishes handed down from the noble families of the court of Savoy. In the cafés in Turin (Torino) you can still see traces of this past opulence in the baroque mirrors and the crystal vases full of tempting *gianduiotti*, hazelnut-flavoured chocolates wrapped in gold paper. Turin could be considered the home of Italian chocolate as it was brought here in the 18th century from France. CIOCCOLATA CALDA is a must, and so are the cakes and pastries.

Before lunch, treat yourselves to an *aperitivo* – Vermouth was invented in Piedmont. Starters come in the form of salads made with slivers of raw meat (CARPACCIO), truffle-flavoured mushrooms, the famous BAGNA CALDA dip or a creamy FONDUTA from the neighbouring Valle d'Aosta. After this rich beginning, you can continue with meat-filled *agnulot* (ravioli) or a winey RISOTTO AL BAROLO or, when the weather is cool, a PANISCIA (thick soup) or a bowl of BRODO (consommé). The Piedmontese prefer to serve their pasta *in brodo* rather than with a sauce. Alba is famous for its TARTUFO BIANCO. Here the restaurants serve their first courses, and most of their main courses, topped with slivers of this unusual strong-tasting 'white' truffle. Meat dishes such as BRASATO AL BAROLO (marinated, braised beef), or game cooked with red wine and mushrooms, are two of the richer main courses, along with FRITTO MISTO (mixed fry), which often includes frogs' legs, cubes of sweet semolina and tiny almond macaroons. As all the ingredients are dipped in batter you cannot tell which is which until you bite into them! Other typical main courses are BOLLITO MISTO IN SALSA VERDE (mixed meats in a green sauce), and trout grilled over a wood fire. A popular summer dish is VITELLO TONNATO (cold veal with tuna mayonnaise) whose origin is contended between Piedmont and Lombardy.

If you can still find a place for a little cheese, try TOMINI or BROSS. The latter, however, is only for lovers of strong flavours! In the country shops and *trattorie* you can find an excellent selection of local salami, buried in lard in earthenware jars, or salted shoulder of pork.

GRISSINI, Italy's world famous bread sticks, first made in Turin in the 17th century, are now an important industry. However, homemade ones of many different widths, lengths and flavours can still be found in bakers' shops.

LOMBARDY

The Lombards are known for being hard workers and not having much time to spend in the kitchen; Lombardy (Lombardia) was the first region to make one-course meals by serving its RISOTTO ALLA MILANESE with

Street café near the shores of Lake Garda

OSSOBUCO. Traditional cookery books, however, contain dishes ranging from the quickly prepared ZUPPA PAVESE (consommé with eggs) to the elaborate CASSOEULA (pork and cabbage casserole) and the famous Christmas bread PANETTONE, taking a whole day to make.

Bergamo and Bréscia serve a lot of POLENTA, either with STRACOTTO (tender cooked beef) or small game birds from the neighbouring valleys. The cattle on the Padua plain not only provide meat for braised and boiled stews but also the excellent dairy produce exported all over the world. Famous cheeses such as GRANA, GORGONZOLA and TALEGGIO are produced, along with the creamy ROBIOLA, STRACCHINO and MASCARPONE (more like a thick clotted cream). The local GRANA (hard cheese) is *parmigianolodigiano* which, they say, is even richer than the world-famous Parmesan cheese, *parmigiano-reggiano*. The ancient town of Mantua (Mantova) is famous for its TORTELLI DI ZUCCA and RISOTTO ALLA MANTOVANA or *alla pilota* (with salami and Parmesan), whereas Cremona makes *torrone* (honey and almond nougat) and MOSTARDA (fruit pickled in mustard sauce).

Across the Padua plain, near Pavia, along the banks of the rivers Ticino and Po, you can find restaurants offering frogs' legs served on a bed of risotto or eels cooked in butter, onions, wine and nutmeg. Dishes of freshwater fish are also found at the lakeside *trattorie* around Lake Como that specialise in

Wild mushrooms. Don't pick your own!

risotto con pesce persico and MISSULTITT (made from salted, dried fish). In the nearby Valtellina valley, the famous PIZZOCCHERI (ribbon pasta) is still served layered with the local BITTO cheese, and BRESAOLA (dried fillet of beef) is served both as a starter and cooked with onions, mushrooms and spices to make *concia*.

All over Lombardy one common denominator prevails in cooking, and that is butter. It was first used for dressing vegetables by Valerio Leonte, a Milanese nobleman, who served *asparagi al burro* to Julius Caesar on his return from Gaul, and it has since been used to dress or sauté vegetables all over the north. Butter is also used to fry COSTALETTA ALLA MILANESE, the veal cutlet which has become a national favourite. The finely minced *luganica* sausage has also found its way all over Italy.

TRENTINO–ALTO ADIGE

The Dolomites mountain range dominates this area of Italy. Dishes such as *polenta carbonara*, made from POLENTA mixed with salami, onions, a strong-flavoured local cheese and 50 grams (2oz) of butter per head, will give you an idea of the type of food to expect – both nourishing and warming. This, together with the rich sauces to accompany game and POLENTA, form the basis of traditional Trentino cooking. Unfortunately, in the tourist season national and international dishes tend to be served in preference to local food. However, one local dish worth seeking out is the sweet-sour *vitello alle mele renette*, a wonderful combination of apples and highly spiced meat. Trentino–Alto Adige is the main apple producing region in Italy, exporting fruit to many parts of the world.

The mild basin around Lake (Lago di) Garda produces citrus fruits and olive oil for summer salads. However, when winter arrives, back comes POLENTA, served with rich sauces made from the wild mushrooms which abound in August and September. Trentino has over 300 lakes, and freshwater fish, such as trout, are on most menus.

In Alto Adige, to the north of Trento, you immediately feel the Austrian influence. German is spoken everywhere, pasta no longer appears on menus, and in its place you find CANEDERLI (smoked ham and sausage dumplings) served in consommé or, like the occasional ravioli, coated in melted butter and Parmesan cheese. Pork, *pancetta* (bacon), WURSTEL (frankfurters) or the smoked SPECK (ham), play a large part in the local cuisine. STINCO DI MAIALE AL FORNO, with its crisp, crunchy, crackling, can be found on most menus, served with boiled or fried potatoes, POLENTA or *crauti* (sauerkraut); and beer is often preferred to wine. Steaks are also served with a spicy onion sauce or coated with cream and mushrooms, Austrian style. The many cake shops reflect the Austrian influence, too, with their tempting chocolate *sachertorte*, fresh fruit tarts with wild strawberries, raspberries and bilberries, and, of course, STRUDEL with apples, nuts and cinnamon.

Rialto fish market, Venice

VENETO

This region, surrounding Venice (Venézia) and its lagoon and stretching inland to the foothills of the Dolomites, has survived on a staple diet of POLENTA since the 16th century, when the maize that is used to make it was first brought to Italy by the Venetian traders.

Risi (*riso*, rice, written in the plural) is peculiar to Veneto where it is cooked to be neither too solid nor too liquid, but *all'onda* – which means it will ripple or 'make waves'. This type of rice, cooked with vegetables, salami, meat, fish or seafood is served as a first course, RISI E BISI being one of the better known dishes. Pasta is used in soups such as *pasta e fas oi* (PASTA E FAGIOLO).

Veneto is also famous for its poultry, fish and offal. FEGATO ALLA VENEZIANA (calves' liver with onion) has become a dish that is popular from Venice down to Sicily. *Baccalà* is served frequently. This is not salted cod (*baccalà*), but dried cod, or STOCCAFISSO. BACCALÀ MANTECATO (dried cod whisked with garlic and olive oil) is one of the most popular ways of serving it, with POLENTA, of course!

Cinque Terre, where the cliffs are cut by steeply terraced vineyards

The Adriatic Sea and the Venetian Lagoon supply Venice and Veneto with fish of all shapes and sizes. These are grilled, baked, fried, stuffed or poached, or made into *brodetto*, the local fish soup. Sardines and sole are marinated in SAOR, a spicy sauce once used to camouflage the taste of fish that was neither too fresh nor of good quality.

Going inland again towards Treviso, poultry in the form of chicken, duck, pigeon, goose, turkey and guinea fowl is served with strongly-flavoured PEVERADA sauce. Treviso is also famous for its RADICCHIO (red-leaved chicory) served as a salad or grilled over a wood/charcoal fire.

Veneto is not without its famous cakes. The Christmas PANDORO comes from Verona, the home of Romeo and Juliet. For anyone who does not have a sweet tooth, bars down Venice's narrow *calli* offer titbits of hard-boiled eggs and tiny crabs to accompany the local wines.

FRIULI-VENEZIA GIULIA

Although famous for its wines, this small region tucked away between Veneto, Austria and Yugoslavia, is not so well known for its food. Foreign influence (Trieste was one of the main ports during the Austrian-Hungarian empire) accounts for the many sweet and sour dishes and savoury food flavoured with cinnamon and sugar, like CIALZONS FRIULANI or CIALZONS ALLA CARNIA (stuffed pasta squares). This unusual sweet and sour combination can also be found in the GNOCCHI served in Trieste, which have a plum hidden in their middle.

Apart from these pasta dishes the people of Friuli enjoy traditional soups made from potatoes, barley, beans and pumpkin, such as JOTA and POLENTA dishes. Friuli has its own sauerkraut called *brovade*, traditionally served with *muset*, a boiled, spiced sausage.

In Carnia, the mountainous region, the characteristic *trattorie* offer regional dishes, some of which originate from Slavic cuisine. They also make FRITTATA CON ERBE (herb omelette), packed with whatever herbs happen to be in season. Half way between the mountains and the coast is San Daniele, the town which gives its name to one of the best cured hams in Italy. It is sweeter than the one from Parma and ideal for serving with melon as a starter.

Down on the coast look for fish risottos and the local *brodetto* (fish soup). Dressed crab (*granseola*) is also a speciality. Cakes and pastries also reflect a foreign influence; GUBANA (sweet bread roll) is of Slavic origin, for example.

LIGURIA

Although Liguria, on the Ligurian Sea in the northwest, is mountainous, allotments abound as the climate is excellent. The local cuisine is therefore based on vegetables and herbs as well as fish. The coast is full of olive groves. The olive oil is so light that it is often enjoyed sprinkled on FOCACCIA (bread-like pizza), with just a little sea salt, to make a delicious snack. It is also used to make a soup called MESCIUÀ (bean, sweetcorn and chick-pea soup).

The Ligurians make savoury cakes and stuffed pizzas, such as TORTA PASQUALINA, served at Eastertime. It is not surprising that PESTO is one of the best known sauces, since basil, which has a particular flavour in Liguria, grows everywhere. It sprouts out of old tin cans on balconies and from terracotta vases on windowsills, as well as being found in gardens and allotments.

Fish is cooked and served in all possible ways. BURIDDA (fish and vegetable stew) and CIUPPIN are both typical fish dishes, and STOCCAFISSO (dried cod), which was the staple diet aboard ship, is cooked in an earthenware casserole with olives, potatoes and pine kernels. The real Ligurian fish masterpiece, however, is CAPPON MAGRO, which must be the richest *maigre* dish (for a day of fasting), in all the cuisine of Italy!

Meat does not play a large part in the Ligurian kitchen. The most characteristic meat dish is CIMA RIPIENA (stuffed veal), with more filling than meat. Eggs, cheese and vegetables are also used to stuff the local RAVIOLI. In Genoa (Genova), visit the *friggitorie* where almost anything is fried in the local olive oil. In the antique-looking cake shops you can sample local specialities made from cocoa, candied peel and almond paste. *Pan dolce*, the Ligurian Christmas cake, is full of pine kernels, pistachio nuts, candied peel and raisins.

EMILIA–ROMAGNA

TORTELLINI (ring-shaped pasta). smothered in cream and cheese, characterise Emilia–Romagna, in north central Italy, where they certainly live to eat and not eat to live! Home-made *pasta all'uovo* (egg pasta) is cut into *tagliatelle* or used to make stuffed pasta, which changes its name according to the filling or place of origin. *Cappelletti* (little pasta hats) are made in Romagna, where one of the filling ingredients is the local *raviggiolo* cheese, whereas in Ferrara they are stuffed with minced brains and turkey breast. Modena is famous for its square-shaped RAVIOLI filled with minced roast meats, while Bologna is the place to find the famous TORTELLINI which, legend has it, were modelled on Venus' navel! *Tortelli* in Piacenza and Parma are filled with RICOTTA cheese and spinach, while in Ferrara they are called *cappellacci* and stuffed with pumpkin and cheese. The main ingredient in classic lasagne is the rich, meaty BOLOGNESE sauce. Emilia is also famous for its cured hams and dried sausages or INSACCATI (meaning 'put in a bag'), like salami, or the pear-shaped *culatello* from Parma, so highly prized that the Marquis of Pallavicini was known to have given them as wedding gifts! Parma is of course better known for its ham, *prosciutto di Parma*. while Modena produces the famous ZAMPONE (a spiced sausage) and MORTADELLA, the luncheon meat which is delicious eaten in a PIADINA ROMAGNOLA (soft, flat bread eaten filled and folded), heated on a griddle at the roadside. *Salama da sugo* (local salami) was served as an aphrodisiac by the ruling Este family and even today can be found at wedding banquets!

The local cheese is, of course, *parmigiano-reggiano* (see GRANA), the world-famous Parmesan that is generously sprinkled over everything except the fish from the Adriatic coast. Again we find the local BRODETTA (this time spelt with two ts) and also seasoned fish coated in breadcrumbs and cooked on the spit, or eels from Comácchio. Rich sweet dishes such as ZUPPA INGLESE (a sort of trifle), or *pan pepato* from Ferrara, a sweet bread crammed with

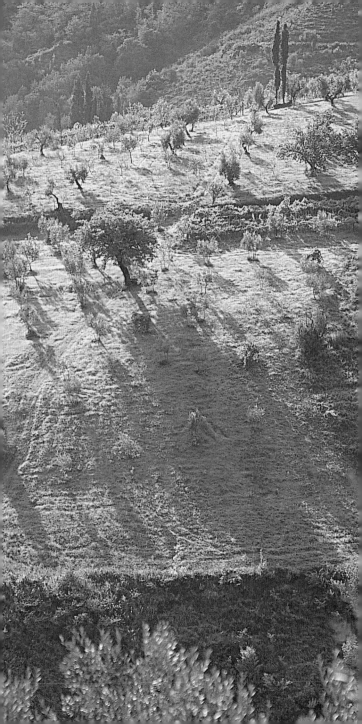

◄ *Lush green olive groves dot the Tuscan landscape*

almonds, walnuts and pine kernels, complete the meal.

TUSCANY

The rolling hills of Tuscany (Toscana), with their green and brown patchwork and gnarled olive trees, are redolent of an Italian way of life which is reflected in the simple, wholesome local cuisine: the famous BISTECCA ALLA FIORENTINA (or just *fiorentina*) – a thick steak grilled over a wood or charcoal fire – being an excellent example.

During the Renaissance Florentine nobles ate lavishly. Ordinary people, however, ate very simply. The most common 'filler' at that time was CASTAGNACCIO, made from chestnut flour and now eaten as a cake. Crusty bread sprinkled with the magnificent Tuscan olive oil with its full, intense flavour was also, and still is, a favourite filler. Pasta is sometimes eaten in the form of PAPPARDELLE AL SUGO DI LEPRE (ribbon pasta with a hare sauce), but more typical first courses are vegetable soups, thick ones such as RIBOLLITA or thin ones like ACQUA COTTA, which is served in the Tuscan Maremma near Grosseto.

Grilled meats of all kinds have pride of place on Italian menus. Beef, lamb, pork, poultry and game are barbecued over a wood or charcoal fire or roasted in the oven, as with the pork dish ARISTA DI MAIALE. Another favourite main course is grilled pigs' liver flavoured with bay leaves. Chicken livers are minced and served on toast as CROSTINI.

Famous cured meats, like the salamis FINOCCHIONA and SOPPRESSATA, are made from pork, but down in the Maremma you can find hams and sausages made from wild boar (CINGHIALE).

Fish dishes such as CACCIUCCO, a fish soup, or TRIGLIE ALLA LIVORNESE (red mullet cooked with chilies), can be found all along the coast, and near Pisa they also specialise in eels cooked with garlic and sage.

Beans are probably the most characteristic vegetable, as Tuscan beans are very versatile. Haricot beans were originally cooked in a Chianti flask. FAGIOLI AL FIASCO can still be found on menus along with fagioli ALL' UCCELLETTO, cooked with tomato and sage. The delicious local cheeses, made from ewes milk, can be bought direct from farms or stalls in markets or at local *feste*. Here you can also find *brigidini* little aniseed cakes cooked on a griddle at the stall.

Most Tuscan restaurants will offer CANTUCCI biscuits and a glass of the sweet Vin Santo to complete your meal, but in Siena you may be offered the local PANPORTE (Christmas cake) or RICCIARELLI (small marzipan cakes) instead.

UMBRIA

This small central region, with its medieval towns of Assisi, Gubbio and Perúgia, offers good, wholesome cooking and delicious grilled meats, very similar to Tuscany's. The olive oil is excellent, though not produced on a large scale, but the 'star' ingredient of Umbrian cuisine is the TARTUFO NERO (black truffle). At weekends, during the summer months, Umbrian villages and towns hold *sagre* (festivals) to venerate the truffle. Black truffle is added in handfuls to sauces, chopped into a paste with anchovies and spread on toast to make *crostini neri*. It is also served with *stringozzi*, a home-made pasta from Spoleto made from flour and water, and added to omelettes and the cheesey bread called PIZZA DI PASQUE. The wild ASPARAGI (asparagus) found in the countryside are made into a cream sauce and served with pasta, added to risottos or served as a vegetable. When in season, they are often an excuse for another *sagra*.

Norcia is famous for its pork and pork products such as SALSICCE (sausages), finoc-chiella (fennel-flavoured salami), LONZA (a lean salami) and MEZZAFEGATO an unusual-tasting pigs' liver sausage. In Rome you can even find shops called *Norcineria* that sell pork, ham and salami. Game-lovers can find wild doves and small birds roasted on the spit with a sauce called *alla* GHIOTTA (*or leccarda*). Another traditional way of cooking chicken, duck or rabbit is IN PORCHETTA.

Even though Umbria has no coastline, you can get fish from the lakes of Trasimeno and Piediluco; and the trout of the Fonti del Clitunno (between Spoleto and Assisi) are just waiting to jump on your line, the lakes are so full!

Biscuits for dipping in wine are again popular, along with cakes made from almonds, glace cherries and nuts. The most unusual cakes are *stinchetti*, tiny marzipan replicas of human tibias (leg bones) which, when eaten, are supposed to fortify and protect the bones!

THE MARCHE

The largest wholesale fish market on the Adriatic coast is in San Benedetto, so fish is obviously one of the main regional foods. The BRODETTO DI PESCE served from Pesaro

Ancient Narni on Umbria's border, a landscape clothed with sunflowers

down to Ancona is made from thirteen varieties of fish cooked in tomato sauce (the superstitious are allowed to add one or two more!), whereas the fish soup from Porto Recanati down to San Benedetto is flavoured with saffron and has no tomatoes. STOCCAFISSO (dried cod) pops up yet again and is cooked with tomatoes and potatoes (called *in potacchio*) which turn it into a real delicacy.

Inland, the traditional first course is VINCIS-GRASSI similar to lasagne. The name, legend says, comes from the distorted local pronun-ciation of Prince 'Windisch-Graetz', a captain in the Austrian army fighting against Napoleon, who apparently tasted this dish while in Ancona. Stuffed pasta is found in Pesaro where *cappelletti in brodo* is a favourite, especially at Christmas time. Home-made *tagliatelle* is served with a rich RAGÙ) and generously sprinkled with grated PECORINO cheese. Near Pesaro you can find RAVIOLI stuffed with ricotta cheese and served, rather unusually, with a fish sauce.

The local olives are large and fleshy, and perfect for turning into OLIVE ASCOLANE (stuffed, fried green olives), which are an essential ingredient in the local FRITTO MISTO ALL'ITALIANA.

ROME AND LAZIO

The typical Roman *osteria* (inn) has its own special character in its decor of plain, painted walls and its wooden tables covered with fresh sheets of paper. It is in these family-run businesses that you can sample the real Roman cooking known as *casalinga* or *casareccia*: unpretentious, plain, home cooking, prepared with first-class local ingre-dients from the fertile countryside of Lazio (Latium). The traditional pasta dishes such as homemade *fettuccine con ragù, rigatoni alla pagliata* (ribbed pasta with calves intestines in a tomato sauce), s*paghetti alla carbonara* and *bucatini all'amatriciana* (thick spaghetti pasta with a tomato and chilli sauce) are all served smothered in grated *pecorino* cheese, The thick pasta and pulse soups

19

such as PASTA E FAGIOLI (with beans), PASTA E LENTICCHIE (with lentils) and PASTA E CECI (with chick-peas) can be found on all *osteria* menus along with the lighter STRACCIATELLA (broth with egg and cheese).

The main courses can be divided into two categories: the more 'sophisticated' lamb dishes, such as ABBACCHIO ARROSTO (roast lamb) and ABBACCHIO ALLA SCOTTADITO (grilled chops) with INVOLTINI DI MANZO (beef rolls) and SALTIMBOCCA ALLA ROMANA (veal escalopes flavoured with ham and sage); and the more down-to-earth offal dishes such as CODA ALLA VACCINARA (oxtail stew), TRIPPA ALLA ROMANA (tripe in a tomato sauce) or the unique PAGLIATA, made from the milk-filled intestines of a suckling calf.

The vegetables are many and varied: broccoli, CICORIA and BROCCOLETTI (the last two being leafy vegetables which can be bitter) are usually sautéed in olive oil with garlic and sometimes chillies. These, with CARCIOFI ALLA ROMANA (artichokes stuffed with

Ewe's and goat's milk are used to make local cheeses in the mountainous region of Abruzzo

garlic and herbs), when in season, are among the most typical. On Sundays, the Romans often go to the country for lunch where a starter of BRUSCHETTA (garlic toast) served with slices of LONZA (a kind of ham or salami) might precede the pasta; or they may pick up some PORCHETTA (stuffed roast pork) from a roadside stall to take on a picnic. Back in Rome, we must not forget the pizzerias, usually crowded on Sunday evenings, serving PIZZA, suppli (fried rice balls) and CROSTINI (savoury toast). Roman pizzas are definitely on a par with those served in Naples, though they are thinner and more biscuity. The bars offer a variety of *tramezzini* (sandwiches) difficult to equal in other parts of Italy, and their MARITOZZI CON LA PANNA (sweet cream-filled buns) make a perfect mid-morning snack.

ABRUZZO AND MOLISE

This mountainous area, which climbs up to Gran Sasso, the highest peak in the Apennines, is a region of sheep farmers. The main course is nearly always lamb, mutton or goat, served grilled, roasted, casseroled, stewed or coated in egg and breadcrumbs and fried. *Agnello arrosto* (roast lamb), *agnello all'arrabbiata* (lamb with tomatoes and chillies) or *agnello cacio e uova* (with egg and cheese) are a few favourites. CAPRETTO (baby goat) is barbecued on the spit or baked in the oven, while the entrails of both lamb and goat are cooked in seasoned tomato sauce and wine. Whole young pigs are roasted to make PORCHETTA. The cheaper offcuts are marinated in a vinegar mixture, then casseroled with chilli to make the famous *'ndocca 'ndocca* from Teramo. PEPER-ONCINO (chillies) are again used in the pasta sauces served with the traditional MACCHERONI ALLA CHITARRA.

Look out for cheeses such as CACIO-CAVALLO and PECORINO, made from ewes' and goats' milk, and do try the SCAMORZA from Rivisondoli. Grilled over a wood fire, it makes a delicious change from meat. Over on the Adriatic coast, in Pescara, you can try *brodetto alla pescarese*, full of chilli of course, and in Vasto they make *scapece*, marinated fish coloured with saffron from L'Aquila.

The Abruzzo is also known for *digestivi* or herb-based liqueurs, of which *Centerbe* is the most famous; most restaurants will put several bottles on the table at the end of the meal. CONFETTI (coloured sugared almonds) are a speciality of Sulmona, and cakes made from almonds and walnuts can be found all over, every town having its own speciality.

CAMPANIA

Tomatoes, grown all over the south of Italy, were first canned and made into purée in Campania. The most common pasta dish is *spaghetti al pomodoro* (with tomato) or *pummarola*, in Neapolitan dialect, but another firm favourite is *spaghetti con aglio e olio* (with garlic and oil). More elaborate sauces, such as RAGÙ NAPOLETANO or beef with onions called LA GENOVESE (which, despite its name – 'the Genoese' – is Neapolitan) are usually made for Sunday lunch. Inland, you can find the traditional MINESTRA MARITATA, a type of soup, and the highly spiced offal dish, SOFFRITTO, which is served with spaghetti or toasted bread. Neapolitans are fond of MINESTRE, thick soups made from pasta and pulses such as beans, chick-peas and lentils. Also popular are pasta with vegetables, like PASTA E PATATE, PASTA E PISELLI and PASTA E CAVOLFIORE, which are so filling they make a one-course meal. An alternative to pasta is SARTÙ DI RISO, a really rich rice pie originating from the reign of the Bourbons. Made on special occasions, it is difficult to find outside the home.

Fish obviously plays a large part in Neapolitan cuisine, especially the octopus and squid caught in the Bay of Naples. ZUPPA DI COZZE, *spaghetti alle vongole veraci* (*vongole veraci* are true clams, a particular, large variety that have small 'horns' protruding from their shells) and POLPI AFFOGATI (octopus in a spicy tomato sauce) are thee most popular dishes, not to mention the delicious roast fish.

The local cheeses, such as PROVOLONE, SCAMORZA and CACIOCAVALLO, are worth tasting, but the real delicacy is the MOZZARELLA DI BUFALA. Around Salerno you can still find *burielli*, mini mozzarella cheeses covered with cream and sold in earthenware jars. (Unfortunately, they would not survive a journey!) Should you be staying in a Neapolitan household, you may be treated to a *pizza rustica*, a pizza-pie filled with anything from greens cooked with garlic, to eggs and salami.

The bars and cake shops sell RUSTICI, with a sweet pastry case and a savoury filling, and TARALLI (savoury, ring-shaped biscuits). The real sweet treats are the SFOGLIATELLE (sweet ricotta-filled cakes) in two versions, either *ricce* or *frolle* (made with puff or short-crust pastry). Should you ever be in Naples at Easter time, you can also try the PASTIERA or, at Christmas, the STRUFFOLI.

Campanian oranges and lemons are some of Italy's best

Contented shepherd on the Gargano Peninsula

APULIA

Apulia (Puglia) was once almost entirely covered with sheep. Now the plain has been claimed for agriculture, mainly cultivation of durum wheat and vegetables. These are then made into pasta and its accompanying vegetable sauces, such as ORECCHIETTE CON CIME DI RAPA (turnip tops), one of the most famous local dishes. Vegetables are also used in the TIELLA (local dialect for *teglia* or baking tin). You can find *tielle* in which ingredients such as sardines or lamb are layered with potatoes and vegetables and baked in the oven. The *tiella di riso e cozze* has the unusual combination of mussels, potatoes and rice.

Apulia, being almost a peninsula, is famous for its fish. The shellfish farms in the Gulf of Taranto produce not only excellent mussels but also the sought-after oyster. The tiny TRIGLIE (red mullet), which live among the rocks along the coast, are really special when barbecued, while the fresh anchovies, when fried and seasoned, can easily compete with the more sophisticated

roast sea bass. Bari, on the Adriatic coast, is famous for its *polpi arricciati* ('curled' octopus), which are subjected to a beating and whirling in special baskets to make them curl.

You cannot leave Apulia without tasting its golden olive oil, which is often thought of as being rather rich by northerners. It is, of course, used generously in all local dishes and in the making of bread and the bread-like pizza FOCACCIA.

The local production of almonds influences the type of cakes and pastries made.

BASILICATA AND CALABRIA

These two mountainous regions, stretching down into the toe of Italy, are known as the 'deep south'. Tourism, unfortunately, has encouraged hotels and restaurants, especially those on the coast, to serve 'national' dishes, You have to go inland to sample traditional regional cuisine, Home-made pasta types, made to old recipes, include *strascinati* (rolled over specially carved boards) and *fusilli* (wrapped around knitting needles to make spirals). They are served with rich RAGÙ sauces, made from chopped lamb, veal and tomatoes and, of course, PEPERONCINO, which is added to everything in handfuls! This habit of highly seasoning everything with chillies dates back to the time when they were eaten whole to ward off illnesses. *Sugna piccante*, made from pork dripping, salt, fennel seeds and lots of chilli, is used for flavouring sauces or soups, or may be just spread on bread, Pork is the main meat, and every bit of the pig is used; even the blood is not wasted, going to make SANGUINACCIO (a dense chocolate spread!). SALSICCE (sausages), spiced with black pepper and chilli, are found everywhere and eaten raw, fried, grilled, roasted, dried, smoked or pickled in olive oil to keep them moist. According to Cicero, the sausage was invented in Basilicata (or Lucania as it is also known); in fact, sausage is often called *luganica*, from 'Lucania'. The CAPOCOLLO, PEZZENTA and SOPPRESSATA, all

Onion picking in Calabria

locally cured meats, are excellent. The other common meat is lamb; and dairy products are made mainly from ewes' milk. RICOTTA, with a salted version called *ricotta forte*, CACIOCAVALLO and PECORINO are the more common cheeses, along with the buttery BUIRRINI.

Down on the coast the fish soup is full of chilli, and an unusual type of 'caviar', called *mestica*, is made from newly hatched anchovies mixed with chilli and oil.

Calabria has its own type of pizza called PITTA, which is stuffed or topped with almost anything, including fish and highly seasoned pork offal. The high plains of the Calabrian Sila range provide delicious mushrooms almost all year round, while the low plains around Santa Eufemia, Sibari and Rosarno produce fruit and vegetables of which the shiny, purple aubergine is the queen.

Locally dried figs, almonds and honey are used to make regional cakes and pastries. *Mostaccioli*, biscuits flavoured with honey and wine, are shaped into saints, fish or animals.

SICILY

Sicily (Sicilia) offers a true Mediterranean cuisine based on olive oil, pasta, fresh fish, fruit, vegetables and herbs. The island is famed for its pasta dishes such as PASTA CON LE SARDE or *pasta alla Norma*, the latter in honour of Vincenzo Bellini, who composed the famous opera *Norma*. The most curious pasta dish, however, is *spaghetti al nero di seppie*, coloured pitch black by cuttlefish ink.

Arab influence can be found in the fish soup from Trápani called *cuscusu*, served with saffron-flavoured semolina. Trápani is probably better known, however, for its fresh tuna, baked, barbecued or fried with onions to make *tonno alla cipollata*. Messina is famous for its PESCE SPADA (swordfish), which are caught in the Straits of Messina. The local dishes are PESCE SPADA ALLA GRIGLIA and PESCE SPADA ALLA GHIOTTA, while the sardines caught all around the island are served as SARDE A 'BECCAFICU' (boned, stuffed and fried).

Meat dishes are less characteristic but the typical FARSU MAGRU (stuffed meat roll) is well worth a mention. Vegetables play a large part in Sicilian cuisine, aubergines and

23

tomatoes taking the leading roles. Together they can be found in the sweet and sour dish CAPPONATA. Sicilians love sweet foods, and their CANNOLI SICILIANI (rolled biscuits filled with ricotta cheese, candied fruit and chocolate), CASSATA SICILIANA (light sponge cake with a ricotta cheese filling) and *fruttini siciliani* (marzipan fruits and vegetables) are famous all over Italy. Lovers of savoury snacks can choose an ARANCINO (rice ball) or get some tasty *pane e meuza* (bread slices or rolls filled with charcoal-grilled pork offal – usually lights – which is highly seasoned, sometimes with chilli) from a street stall in the old town and then move on for a freshly squeezed SPREMUTA (fruit juice).

SARDINIA

In the mountainous regions of Sardinia (Sardegna) the people still live mainly as shepherds, while on the coast the tourist yachts lie anchored. Crayfish or lobster

Sicilian olive grove – the best olives are hand-picked to make the finest olive oil

dominate the coastal menus, but traditional dishes are found inland, where even the bread is made to suit the shepherd's needs – it is thin, crisp and it breaks easily, ideal for carrying into the fields in quantity and unlikely to become stale quickly. Bread-making is one of the oldest traditions in Sardinia, where special bread is shaped into animals, flowers, or churches for weddings, into lace for christenings and is made from wholemeal flour for funerals as a sign of mourning. PORCEDDU (suckling pig) is barbecued 'shepherd style' over a wood fire. For a *festa*, larger animals were sometimes roasted whole, one inside the other like Russian dolls, in a pit dug in the ground. Unfortunately, it is difficult to find barbecued meats, apart from lamb, along the tourist track. The cured meats, however, are more accessible as they can be bought in the village stores. Hams are made from pork or wild boar, and the local sausage, highly peppered and flavoured with fennel seeds and wine vinegar, is hung next to the fireplace to be lightly smoked. It can be eaten raw, grilled or, cooked in tomato sauce, served with the small ribbed pasta shells called MALLOREDDUS. Local cheeses such as *fiore sardo* or fresh ROCOTTA are naturally made from ewes' milk.

Many typical fish dishes were brought to Sardinia by invaders; for instance, the fish soup found in Cagliari called CASSOLA is of Spanish origin. BURIDDA, which in Genoa is a soup, here becomes fish poached in vinegar solution and topped with nuts. A typical Sardinian speciality is BOTTARGA (salted and dried fish roes), offered as a starter or crumbled over spaghetti. Sardinian sweets are easily found, SEADAS (a kind of cheese tart) or individually wrapped almond *sospiri* are often served in tourist restaurants, whereas *pabassinas*, iced sultana cakes decorated with coloured sugar strands, can be bought in supermarkets.

Sardinian shepherds may be encountered along the lonely mountain roads

A–Z of Italian Food

A

Abbacchio   ✪✪✪
Roman spring lamb. In other parts of Italy it is called AGNELLO. Slaughtered between three and 12 months old, they are very tender, being still unweaned. A whole animal may weigh as little as 5kg/10lb. In Rome, there are special butchers' shops selling only lamb, chicken and eggs, called *abbacchi e poli*; here lamb carcases are hung from the ceiling waiting to be sold whole, cut in half or by the kilo.

Abbacchio alla cacciatora   ✪✪✪
Hunter-style lamb, a Roman dish. It is chopped into small pieces and cooked in olive oil, garlic and rosemary, then sprinkled with wine vinegar.

Abbacchio alla scottadito   ✪✪✪
Tender chops, grilled over a wood or charcoal fire. They are meant to be picked up and eaten with your fingers – carefully, or you will do as their name suggests and 'burn your finger'!

Abbacchio arrosto   ✪✪✪
Lamb roasted in the oven with rosemary and garlic. It is a typical Roman dish, a favourite for Sunday lunch, especially at Easter time. Legs or shoulders of lamb are roasted whole, cut into portions and served on the bone. The meat is so tender that it melts in your mouth.

Acciughe
Anchovy fillets. Used to flavour and garnish pizzas and to enrich many fish-based sauces. Also delicious served with butter and crackers or bread as a starter. Anchovies can be bought ready prepared in small bottles or cans, but the best ones are those still under salt at the grocer's. Rinse them in a little vinegar to remove the salt, then serve them in olive oil with chopped garlic and oregano.

Aceto di vino
Wine vinegar. There are many different types of wine vinegar available, some of which are flavoured with herbs. Most house-holds make their own wine vinegar by keeping a special bottle where they pour the dregs of their wine. The presence of a small piece of pasta ensures that the wine turns into vinegar. It is difficult to find malt vinegar.

Acqua cotta   ✪✪✪
Thin vegetable soup made from onions, garlic, celery, carrots, peppers and tomatoes, served in terracotta bowls lined with croûtons. It is sometimes served with an egg poached in it. This dish from the Tuscan Maremma is really warming on cold days.

Aglio
Garlic. Used extensively in Italian cooking, garlic-sellers can always be found in the markets with their strings of the pungent bulb to hang in the kitchen. Garlic does not last forever, however, and tends to turn into mould if not kept in a cool, dry place.

Agnello
Lamb.

Agnello al forno or tiella di agnello   ✪✪
Spring lamb, cut into chunks and baked in the oven with potatoes, onions, tomatoes, garlic, olive oil and white wine and seasoned with ground black pepper and oregano. This way of roasting lamb is typical of Naples and the south.

Agnolotti   ✪
Squares of freshly made pasta. Similar to ravioli, they are usually stuffed with ricotta cheese and spinach. They are sometimes stuffed with meat, especially in the north, and are then usually served in a tomato and basil sauce.

Agrodolce
Sweet and sour. Vegetables such as red peppers, onions and courgettes are sometimes served in this way, cooked in a vinegar solution with the addition of sugar. They are then glazed with the sauce before serving.

A love of garlic and peppers is an advantage in Italy

Seafood salad, a tasty way to start your meal

Albicocche
Apricots. They are in season for most of the summer. The larger ones, despite their deliciously tempting appearence, are sometimes quite tasteless and it is often better to select the smaller fruit. When buying for apricots ask if you can choose your own; most shopkeepers will be happy to oblige, especially in the south.

Alici
Fresh anchovies.

Alici dorate e fritte   ✪✪✪
Fresh anchovies, dipped in seasoned flour and beaten egg, then fried in olive oil until golden. They are served with wedges of lemon and a crisp green salad. A delicious but cheap fish dish.

Amarene
Sour cherries. Used to make jams and the deliciously thick syrup or conserve that is sometimes poured over vanilla ice-cream.

Amaretti   ✪
Bitter almond macaroons. Sometimes served with drinks or used for making cakes and desserts. They are also one of the unusual ingredients in the FRITTO MISTO served in Piedmont.

Amatriciana, all'   ✪✪✪
Sauce made with tomatoes, bacon, onion and chillies. Traditionally served with BUCANTI (spaghetti-like pasta) and sprinkled with grated pecorino cheese (see recipe on page 104).

Ananas
Pineapple.

Anatra in porchetta   ✪✪
Duck stuffed with finely chopped duck's liver, bacon or ham, rosemary, garlic and fennel. It is roasted in the oven, basted with white wine, until tender. Often found in Tuscany and Umbria.

Anellini
Small pasta rings served in BRODO.

Anguilla
Freshwater eel. Found in most rivers and lakes, *anguille* are cooked in many different ways depending on local tradition. They can either be seasoned with various herbs and spices and cooked in chunks on the spit, or casseroled with or without tomatoes. *Anguille* are bred in abundance in the Comácchio Valley where they are one of the traditional regional dishes.

Anguilla alla comácchio   ✪✪✪
Skinned eel cooked in a pan with chopped onion, rosemary and a sprinkling of vinegar.

Tomatoes and seasoning are then added. When the eel is cooked and the sauce thick, it is served with POLENTA.

Anguria ✪✪✪

Watermelon. These vary on size and shape from the smaller, dark green round ones, weighing approximately 2kg/4lb, to the larger, oblong yellow and green striped ones, weighing up to 10kg/20lb each. From June through to September, enormous piles of watermelons appear at the roadsides up and down the country. They are guarded 24 hours a day by watermelon vendors, sleeping in rough shacks built among the fruit. Watermelons are also sold by the slice on street stalls in the cities, cooled with blocks of ice. *'Mangi, bevi e ti lavi la faccia!'* 'You eat, drink and wash your face!" – a good Italian description of consuming this refreshing fruit!

Antipasto

Hors d'oeuvres. There are many different types of *antipasto*, or starters, ranging from the *antipasto all'italiana* or *antipasto misto* – a selection of sliced meats and cheeses, served with olives, pickles and anchovy fillets (see recipe on page 103) – to the more sophisticated fish and seafood salads. Some of the more common are: BRUSCHETTA, INSALATA DI MARE, OLIVE ASCOLANE, *piatto freddo* (similar to *antipasto all'italiana*), PROSCIUTTO E MELONE and *tartine al tartufo* (canapés with truffles).

Aragosta ✪

Crayfish. Although the dictionary translation is crayfish, many people mistakenly call it lobster. Sardinia is the main Italian producer of *aragosta* but, even there, it is still expensive. When fresh, crayfish are delicious poached and served simply with olive oil and lemon or mayonnaise. Most fish restaurants keep their crayfish alive in tanks of seawater and customers are invited to choose their own.

Arance

Oranges. An orange tree, laden with bright orange fruit hanging among the dark green leaves, is a wonderful sight when spotted for the first time. Another memorable experience is the penetrating perfume of the orange groves in blossom in spring, at sunset. Italy produces oranges of all types, from the juicy *tarocchi* with thin, shiny peel,

and the *sanguinelle* (blood oranges) to the extra sweet *vaniglia* (vanilla oranges) that come from Sicily. The first oranges start to arrive in the markets in November and last right through winter and spring.

Arancini ✪✪✪

Savoury rice balls. They are not always round being sometimes shaped like a pointed orange. They are made from boiled rice mixed with butter and grated Parmesan cheese, left to cool and then moulded into shape. A spoonful of rich meat sauce and peas is put in the middle of each ball, which is then coated in egg and breadcrumbs and fried. Found in most bars and *rosticcerie* in Sicily, where they are a delicious traditional snack.

Arista di maiale ✪

Boned loin of pork, seasoned with garlic, rosemary and fennel. The name of the dish comes from the Greek *arista*, meaning 'the best'. The meat is either roasted in the oven or on the spit. Most restaurants serve slices of it with potatoes roasted in the same tin. This delicious Tuscan main course can also be found in other parts of central and northern Italy.

Arrabbiata, all' ✪✪✪

Sauce made with tomatoes, oil, garlic and lots of chillies. Traditionally served with PENNE (pasta quills) and sprinkled with chopped parsley. Very spicy, it is recommended for curry lovers (see recipe on page 109).

Arrosto misto ✪

Mixed roast meats. Compared to some of the other exciting items on the menu, this dish may look rather boring. However, when it includes crispy golden piglet, tender spring lamb, roast veal and one or two local sausages it competes very well. This is especially the case when all the meats, fragrantly seasoned with herbs, have been barbecued over glowing embers and kept moist by basting with wine throughout the cooking.

Arrosto in casseruola ✪

Pot roast. A lean piece of young beef or veal is cooked with oil, butter and wine on a bed of chopped onions, carrots, celery and mushrooms. These vegetables form the sauce served with pasta as a first course. This dish is usually made at home.

Asiago ⊗

A cheese produced in the north of Italy on the high plain of Asiago. It has a spongy appearance (it is full of tiny holes) and a mild flavour and is made in large round cheeses that are cut to order.

Asparagi

Asparagus. Despite Italy being one of the main producers of asparagus, the price never seems to fall very low. At its best in April and May, it is sold in the shops and markets tied in bundles. Asparagus is usually served boiled and dressed with olive oil and lemon juice or topped with a fried egg. It is also used in risottos, pasta sauces and omelettes.

Asparagi alla parmigiana ⊗

Asparagus coated with melted butter and grated Parmesan cheese. This rich dish is from Emilia-Romagna.

Astice

Lobster. This is the real lobster with its two large nippers, as opposed to crayfish. See ARAGOSTA for serving suggestions.

Fresh asparagus bundles at L'Aquila market

B

Baccalà alla vicentina ⊗⊗⊗

Dried cod (STOCCAFISSO) simmered with onions and milk for several hours until the sauce becomes thick and creamy. It is then served with slices of fried POLENTA.

Baccalà mantecato ⊗⊗

Dried cod (STOCCAFISSO) whisked with garlic and olive oil to form a thick creamy paste. Served cold with toast or POLENTA. This unusual strong-flavoured dish from Veneto, is not to everyone's taste.

Baccalà ⊗⊗⊗

Salted cod. These strong-smelling fillets are found all over Italy. On Fridays, a traditional 'fish' day, you can buy them already soaked, ready to be transformed into one of the many regional dishes that include them. Coated in batter and deep fried as crunchy *filetti di baccalà*, they are served in Roman pizzerias. In Veneto, dried cod (STOCCAFISSO) is called *baccalà* (with one 'c'), which can cause confusions. However, the two kinds of cured fish (salted and dried) are very similar.

Bagna calda ⊗⊗⊗

An oily dip strongly flavoured with garlic and anchovies. It is served in a special pot, over a burner, placed in the centre of the table, with a selection of raw and cooked vegetables. In Piedmont these 'dipped' vegetables, served with crusty bread, make a good starter or light lunch.

Bagnet

Sauces in Piedmont, served with boiled meats, fish or eggs.

Bagnet di pomodori ⊗

A sieved tomato sauce spiced with chillies and vinegar.

Bagnet verde ⊗

Sauce made from chopped parsley, anchovy fillets and garlic, mixed with breadcrumbs, vinegar and oilve oil.

Banane

Bananas.

Basilico

Basil. Fresh basil is used extensively in

Italian cooking and is readily obtainable from greengrocers from spring through to late autumn. The ideal herb for dressing tomatoes and the basis of PESTO GENOVESE.

Bel Paese ☻
A cheese with a mild taste and creamy texture. The round, flat cheese from Lombardy are wrapped in foil depicting a map of Italy, the *bel paese* (beautiful country).

Bignè ☻
Cream puffs filled with custard cream or ZABAIONE. They are found in all cake shops, in various flavours and sizes.

Bignè di San Giuseppe ☻☻☻
Similar to BIGNÈ, but fried, filled with custard cream and dredged with icing sugar. Traditionally, they are eaten to celebrate St Joseph's day on 19 March, but they start appearing in the shops soon after New Year.

Bigoli
A special type of spaghetti, using hard-wheat, wholemeal flour, made from an old recipe handed down from the housewives of Bassano del Grappa.

Biscotti
Biscuits.

Bistecca
Beef steaks from various cuts, such as sirloin, T-bone and rump.

Bistecca alla fiorentina ☻☻
T-bone steak from Tuscany. To be *alla fiorentina*, the meat should come from the Chianina herd (known for their size and the quality meat they yeald), be about 2.5cm/1 inch thick, weigh between 500–800g/1–1¾lb and be grilled over a wood or charcoal fire.

Bistecca alla pizzaiola ☻
A rump or sirloin steak cooked in tomato and oregano sauce similar to that used for pizzas, hence this description, *alla pizzaiola* – 'in the style of the pizza-maker'. Originates from Naples (see recipe on page 109).

Bitto ☻☻
A cheese from the Valtellina valley in Lombardy, made from a mixture of cows' and goats' milk. It has a firm texture and slightly 'musty' flavour. Look out for it in the local shops and markets.

Bocconcini di vitello ☻
Small, bite-sized pieces of veal cooked in wine and butter or oil. Often served with peas or mushrooms.

Bollito misto ☻
A plate of mixed boiled meats from Trentino and Piedmont. These meats include chicken, knuckle of veal, beef, ox tongue and sausage, all sliced and served with boiled potatoes and onions. *Salsa verde* (green sauce), made from chopped parsley, basil, garlic and capers, is the traditional accompaniment to this interesting option for the out-of-season traveller.

Bolognese, alla ☻☻☻
Sauce made with tomatoes, minced beef, carrot, celery and onion. Traditionally served with fresh pasta and grated Parmesan.

Bonet ☻☻
Delicious chocolate-flavoured milk puddings. They contain crushed bitter almond macaroons and are coated with a caramel sauce. A real treat for sweet-toothed visitors to Piedmont.

Borlotti
A type of bean that can be dried, canned or found fresh in the summer. Mottled red and white, they turn brown on cooking, and are used for pasta soups or as a vegetable.

Boscaiola, alla ☻☻
Woodcutter's sauce. This varies from region to region but usually contains mushrooms and ham.

Borlotti *beans, a good substitute for vegetables*

Bottarga ✪✪✪
Salted, dried and pressed tuna fish or mullet roes from Sardinia. Sliced very thinly and served as a starter, or crumbled over spaghetti, it has a very strong 'fishy' flavour.

Braciola di maiale ✪
Loin pork chop, either fried with garlic and fennel seeds or grilled over a wood or charcoal fire.

Brasato al Barolo ✪✪✪
A lean joint of beef marinated overnight (an old recipe recommends eight days!) in red BAROLO wine, herbs and spices, then braised slowly until tender. The meat and its deliciously rich sauce is served in Piedmont with potato purée or POLENTA (see recipe on page 108).

Bresaola ✪✪✪
Dried fillet of beef from the Valtellina valley in the Italian Alps. It is served sliced thinly, dressed with olive oil, lemon juice, ground black pepper and parsley. Served with crusty bread, it makes a delicious starter or even a main course in the summer.

Broccoletti ✪✪
A dark green, leafy vegetable similar to turnip tops. It can sometimes be rather bitter, but is delicious served cold with oilve oil and lemon juice or sautéed with garlic and chillies.

Brodetto di pesce ✪✪✪
Fish soup. It varies, in content and name, from region to region. In Veneto it is called brodeto, while in the south it is ZUPPA DI PESCE, which usually includes shellfish.

Brodetto di pesce alla marchigiana ✪✪✪
Fish soup from the Marches. It is made from up to 16 different types of fish, cooked with stock, tomatoes, fennel and a dash of vinegar and served with croûtons.

Brodo ✪
A thin meat broth or consommé. Served as a soup with small pasta shapes (pastina) or stiffed pasta (TORTELLINI), or used to make risottos.

Bross ✪✪
A sort of 'potted' cheese from Piedmont. A mixture of local cheese is creamed together with GRAPPA and wine spread on bread.

Bruschetta ✪✪✪
Garlic toast. This is a typical Roman starter. Delicious eaten piping hot with sliced, cured ham and accompanied by a glass of cool

wine from the Castelli Romani (see recipe on page 103).

Brutti e buoni ✪✪
Small almond rock cakes found in Umbria and Tuscany. They are called 'ugly and good' because, despite their ugly appearance, they are delicious!

Bucatini
Type of pasta, similar to spaghetti but with a hole running through the centre. Known as perciatelli in the south.

Budino ✪
This milk pudding is similar to blancmange and is usually flavoured with chocolate or vanilla. A favourite with children.

Buridda ✪✪✪
A fish dish. In Liguria it is a stew, dating back to the Saracens, made from mixed fish cooked in tomato sauce with vegetables, anchovy fillets and pine kernels. In Sardinia, however, it is a dish of tuna or rock salmon steaks topped with a mixture of breadcrumbs, chopped nuts, garlic and nutmeg.

Burrini or butirri ✪✪
Small CACIOCAVALLO cheeses from the south with butter in their centre.

Burro, al ✪
Freshly cooked pasta mixed with butter and a little pasta water and served with grated Parmesan. Hardly ever appears on menus, but can always be asked for in restaurants. Simple but delicious when made well.

Busecca ✪✪✪
A Milanese dish made from tripe. The tripe is cut into wafer thin strips, sautéed in butter with vegetables and sage until tender; then cooked large white butter beans are added. Served generously sprinkled with grated Parmesan and black pepper.

C

Cacciatora, alla
'Hunter style'. Meat, such as lamb, chicken or rabbit, cooked with olive oil, garlic and rosemary, and sprinkled with wine vinegar.

Cacciucco ✪✪✪
A rich fish soup from Leghorn (Livorno) in Tuscany. Fish, molluscs and shellfish are casseroled with tomatoes, garlic, chillies and red wine. It is served on a bed of croûtons in individual terracotta bowls. Delicious!

Fine Caciocavallo *cheeses from the Basilicata region in the deep south*

Cachi ✪

Persimmons. Pronounced *kakkee*, these are an unusual, very sweet fruit with a rather 'slimy' texture. They are in season in late summer.

Cacio e pepe ✪✪

A simple sauce made from grated pecorino cheese and lashings of freshly ground black pepper.

Cacio e uova ✪✪

With cheese and egg. Beaten egg and grated cheese are added to vegetables such as courgettes (*zucchini cacio e uova*) or to lamb (*agnello cacio e uova*), while hot, to make a thick coating sauce.

Caciocavallo ✪

Pear-shaped cows' milk cheese from the south. Their name comes from the practice of stringing them together in pairs and hanging them *a cavallo* (astride) over wooden beams to mature. Their flavour varies from mild to strong, depending on maturity. See also BURRINI.

Caciotta ✪
Cheese made from ewes' milk. They have a mild flavour and a softish texture. Excellent eaten with olives.

Calamari
Squid. When preparing this popular, though strange-looking mollusc, be careful to remove the head, eyes, transparent cartilage and ink sack (full of very black ink) before cooking. Sold whole or sliced into rings, it is cooked in tomato sauce, grilled or fried.

Calamari fritti ✪✪✪
Deep fried squid. Rings and tentacles of squid are dipped in a light batter and deep fried. Though rather 'rubbery' to the bite they have an interesting fishy taste. They are often served mixed with fried prawns.

Calamari ripieni ✪✪
Stuffed squid. The squid is stuffed with a mixture of breadcrumbs, parsley, garlic, anchovies and capers, then cooked in olive oil and white wine.

Delicious baked, stuffed cannelloni

Calzoni ✪✪✪
A type of pizza. It is folded in half and filled with cooked ham or salami, mozzarella and ricotta cheese, then baked in the oven. Often preferred by Italians as an alternative to pizza.

Canederli ✪✪✪
Small, light dumplings. Made from breadcrumbs flavoured with smoked ham and sausage, they are cooked and served in consommé in Trentino-Alto Adige. Really warming on a cool evening.

Cannellini
Small, white haricot beans which are dried, canned or found fresh in the summer. They are both used as a vegetable and made into delicious soups with pasta.

Cannelloni ✪
Freshly-made rolls of pasta stuffed with various fillings, coated with sauce and baked in the oven. The commonest version has a minced beef filling, is coated with bolognese sauce, topped with white sauce and sprinkled with grated Parmesan. Can easily make a filling one-course meal followed by a salad.

Cannoli siciliani ✪✪✪
Crisp fried rolls that look like brandy snaps. A Sicilian delight, they are filled with sweetened ricotta cheese, candied peel and pieces of chocolate. Except in the really hot months of July and August, they can be bought from most good cake shops.

Cantucci ✪
Nut-filled biscuits, served with a glass of Vin Santo (sweet wine) after a meal in Tuscany.

Capellini
Very fine spaghetti. It is usually served to children in tomato sauce or broken into consommé.

Capitone ✪
Sea-water eel. Found in the south, it is traditionally cooked in tomato sauce and eaten in Naples at Christmas.

Capocollo ✪✪
A Calabrian salami. It is made with cuts of pork from the neck and shoulder, smoked inside a pig's bladder and pickled in olive oil. Delicious, especially when home-made.

Caponata ✪✪✪
A Sicilian sweet and sour dish. In its simplest form, it is made from aubergines and tomatoes mixed with capers, pine kernels, sultanas and olives, and flavoured with vinegar and sugar. It can be 'dressed up' to include even lobster. Served both hot and cold.

Capperi
Capers. The pickled flower buds of a bush-like shrub that grows wild on rock faces exposed to the sun. Capers can be pickled in either vinegar or salt, but in the latter case they must be rinsed well before using. Used to flavour many Italian sauces.

Cappon magro ✪✪
Ornate fish and vegetable dish. This bed of diced vegetables, piled high with poached fish coated in green sauce, garnished with hard-boiled eggs, pickles, artichokes and peeled shrimps and topped with a whole crayfish and a dozen or so oysters, has to be seen to be believed! A traditional *maigre* (for days of fasting) dish from Liguria.

Capretto
Baby goat.

Capretto arrosto ✪✪
Roast baby goat. In this typical dish from the south, the goat is cut into small pieces and baked (although *arrosto* means roasted) in the oven with potatoes, onions, tomatoes, peas and wine. Eaten at Easter.

Caramelle
Sweets.

Carbonade ✪✪✪
Salted beef dish from Valle d'Aosta. The beef is cooked in wine and onions, seasoned with grated nutmeg and served with POLENTA. Called *carbonade* because it is as black as charcoal. Unfortunately it is often made from fresh beef nowadays.

Carbonara, alla ✪✪✪
Piping hot spaghetti mixed with beaten eggs, grated Parmesan and pecorino cheeses, freshly ground black pepper and crunchy, fried chopped bacon. A 'must' for bacon and egg lovers who find themselves in Rome.

Carciofi
Artichokes. These are a very common spring vegetable, eaten from February or March through to May when they are young. The hairy choke will not have developed inside the bud, so preparation is simple compared to the method used for mature artichokes. The outside leaves are pulled off and discarded, then the remaining leaves and stalk are trimmed; the rest is ready for cooking and eating. Choose those that are firm and not too open and 'spiky'.

Carciofi alla Giudia ✪✪✪
Jewish-style artichokes. A speciality of the restaurants in the old Jewish ghetto in Rome, they are opened out like a flower, plunged into boiling oil, then served crisp and piping hot. They literally melt in your mouth.

Carciofi alla romana ✪✪✪
Roman-style artichokes. They are stuffed with garlic, parsley and mint, then braised until tender.

Carciofi dorati e fritti ✪✪
Wedges of artichokes, dipped in flour and beaten egg, then fried in olive oil.

Carne
Meat.

Carpaccio ✪
Paper-thin slices of raw beef dressed with lemon juice and olive oil and served with slivers of Parmesan cheese and RUGHETTA. Do not be put off because the meat is raw – it is really delicious.

Cartoccio
Food baked in foil or a sealed bag.

Cassata siciliana ✪✪✪
A Sicilian dessert made from sweetened ricotta cheese, candied peel and chocolate chips on a sponge base, covered with green almond paste and icing. The dessert is decorated with whole glacé fruits. Extremely sweet but delicious.

Cassoeula ✪✪✪
An ancient Milanese dish made from spare ribs of pork and cabbage casseroled with vegetables. Served with POLENTA. It is traditionally eaten in winter, especially on 17 January, to celebrate St Anthony's Day (he apparently kept pigs!).

Cassola ✪✪✪
An unusual fish soup, found in Cagliari on Sardinia. Made from fish and octopus

Chanti chestnuts are grown in abundance throughout Tuscany

casseroled with dried tomatoes, onions, garlic and chillies, it is served on croûtons in individual dishes.

Castagnaccio ✪
A traditional Tuscan cake made from chestnut flour, pine kernels and sultanas. It is baked in large flat tins and cut into slices.

Castagne
Chestnuts. In the autumn, chestnut sellers sit on street corners with glowing braziers and sell bags of roasted chestnuts. Chestnuts are also used for making cakes and are sometimes served as a vegetable.

Castagnole ✪
Tiny balls of fried dough coated in castor sugar and sometimes filled with custard cream. One of the many sweets served at *carnevale* time (before Lent).

Castrato ✪
Mutton. Served as grilled chops or as the stew, with vegetables and tomatoes, which makes the thick sauce served to accompany pasta in the Marches, Abruzzo and Lazio.

Cavolfiore
Cauliflower. Best in wintertime.

Ceci ✪
Chick-peas, either dried or canned. They are flavoured with rosemary and served as a vegetable in some parts of central Italy, and with pasta in Rome. Friday is the traditional day for *pasta e ceci* in the Roman *osterie*.

Cervella ✪
Calves' brains. They are either sautéed in butter or cut into bite-seized pieces and coated with batter, then fried. Can be found in FRITTO MISTO or sometimes served with fried artichokes.

Charlotte ✪
Dessert made from very light sponge cakes and sandwiched together with freshly whipped cream. One of the most common sweets served in restaurants.

Chiacchiere ✪✪
Strips of dough-like pastry, coated in honey and icing sugar. Traditionally served at *carnevale* time (before Lent).

Take your pick – Italy is a heaven for fish lovers

Chiodini ✪✪
Small mushrooms with a long stalk and tiny head – hence their name, 'little nails'. They grow in mountain valleys, and are delicious served as a vegetable, with pasta or pickled in oil and vinegar.

Cialzons alla Carnia ✪✪✪
Sweet and sour AGNOLOTTI (pasta squares) from Friuli, served as a first course. Stuffed with spinach mixed with chocolate, saltanas and candied peel!

Cialzons frulani ✪✪✪
Sweet and sour AGNOLOTTI (pasta squares) from Friulu, stuffed with mashed potatoes flavoured with cinammon, sugar, parsley and mint. Served with melted butter and grated cheese.

Ciambelle or ciambelline ✪
Ring-shaped home-made biscuits, usually made with wine. They are often served in *trattorie* at the end of a meal and are excellent dipped in wine.'Dunking' is not frowned upon in Italy!

Cicoria ✪✪
A dark green, leafy vegetable with a rather bitter taste. It can be found growing wild in fields. Served sautéed in oil and garlic or cooked in tomato sauce, it is a Roman speciality.

Ciliege
Cherries.

Cima ripiena ✪
A 'pocket' of veal stuffed with beaten egg, cheese and vegetables from Liguria. Served sliced, hot or cold.

Cinghiale ✪✪✪
Wild boar. They abound in the Tuscan Maremma where they are served barbecued, stewed in tomato sauce and served with pasta, or made into hams, salami and sausages. The meat has a stronger flavour than pork, but should be tried.

Cioccolatini
Chocolates. Italy has an excellent reputation for its chocolates, which are exported all over the world. Some of the more interesting ones to try are *Baci* or 'kisses', with chopped hazelnuts; *Gianduiotti*, creamy hazelnut flavoured truffled chocolates; *Kinder*, milk chocolate fingers with a creamy white filling, which children love; and *Pocket Coffee* filled with liquid coffee.

Ciociara, alla ✪✪
Sauce made with cream, mushrooms, chopped cooked ham and peas. Traditionally served with ribbon-shaped pasta.

Onions hung out to dry ready for market

Cipolle
Onions.

Ciuppin ✪✪✪
A sieved fish soup from Liguria, similar to the French *bouill-abaisse*.

Cocco
Coconut. It heralds the arrival of summer with its appearance on street stalls, where it is sold in slices stacked under a 'fountain' of running water to keep it fresh.

Cocomero
The Roman name for ANGURIA (watermelon).

Coda alla vaccinara ✪✪
Oxtail stew. A real Roman dish found in the *osterie* around Testaccio (the area near the old slaughter-house) that specialise in offal dishes.

Colomba ✪
Dove-shaped cake, flavoured with candied peel and covered in flaked almonds and sugar. It is a traditional Easter treat.

Conchiglie
Pasta shells served with tomato and cream-based sauces.

Confetti
Coloured sugared almonds. They play an important part in Italian's social lives. These variously coloured sugared almonds are tied in small decorated bundles and given to friends and relations on special occasions. For first communions and weddings they are white, for wedding anniversaries silver and gold, for engagements green and for graduations red.

Coniglio all'ischitana ✪✪✪
A traditional rabbit dish from Ischia. On this island in the Bay of Naples there would seem to be more hunters than fishermen! The rabbit, after being marinated over night in the local wine, is cooked with tomatoes and chillies until tender, then served with chipped potatoes.

Cornetto ✪✪
A crescent-shaped sweet bread roll, or 'croissant', served for breakfast with *cappuccino*. It owes its name to its 'horn-like' shape.

Costata di manzo
Entrecôte of beef or rib steak

Costoletta alla milanese ✪✪✪
Famous egg and breadcrumbed veal cutlet from Milan. It was invented during the Italian Renaissance when it was the fashion for the rich to have their food served covered with slivers of gold. The poor dipped their cutlets in egg and bread-crumbs, then fried them in butter until golden – in colour at least! This was copied by the Austrians to make *Wienerschnitzel*. This cutlet is now often served without its traditional bone (see recipe on page 110).

Costoletta alla valdostana ✪✪
Veal cutlet with cheese stuffing. Similar to its Milanese cousin, the cutlet is, however, first stuffed with FONTINA cheese, from the Valle d'Aosta, which makes a deliciously creamy centre.

Confetti *has been made in Sulmona, Abruzzo since the 15th century*

Costoletta di agnello/ abbacchio ✪✪

Small lamb chops. They are either grilled or coated in egg and breadcrumbs and deep fried.

Cotechino ✪✪

A type of spicy minced pork sausage. It is normally boiled and served sliced with lentils.

Cotoletta alla bolognese ✪✪

A thin slice of veal, coated with egg and breadcrumbs and fried, then covered with a slice of ham and cheese, topped with tomato sauce and baked in the oven. A very rich dish in true *bolognese* style.

Cozze, alle ✪✪

Sauce made with mussels, with or without tomatoes. Served with spaghetti and parsley.

Crema di. . ., alla ✪✪✪

A cream-based sauce. It can be made from asparagus (*crema di asparagi*), mushrooms (*crema di funghi*), walnuts (*crema di noci*), prawns (*crema di scampi*) or smoked salmon (*crema di salmone*). Usually served with fresh, ribbon-shaped pasta such as *tagliatelle* or *tagliolini*.

Crema fritta ✪✪✪

Fried custard. A Venetian dessert of shapes of thick, chilled, creamy custard, dipped in flour and fried, then dusted with sugar.

Crespelle or crêpes ✪✪

Savoury pancakes filled with a mixture of ricotta and spinach, cooked with tomato sauce and baked in the oven. They are an alternative to pasta. Ham, cheese and meat are also used for fillings.

Crocchette di patate ✪

Fried potato croquettes. Sometimes with mozzarella cheese in the centre, they can be bought in most *pizzerie*. A tasty snack while waiting for pizza.

Crostata di frutta ✪

Fresh fruit tart. The fruit is so beautifully arranged in the open pastry case that these tarts are hard to resist in the cake shop window.

Crostini ✪✪

Savoury toasts. Crusty slices of bread covered with sliced mozzarella cheese and either Parma ham or anchovy fillets, then popped under the grill. Served in *pizzerie* as fillers.

D

Diavola, alla

Devilled. A common way of serving chicken. The chicken is halved, flattened, seasoned with herbs and ground chilli, then grilled or 'devilled' over a wood or charcoal fire.

Ditalini

Small pasta thimbles. Usually served with thick soups.

F

Fagiano

Pheasant.

Fagioli

Dried haricot or cannellini beans.

Fagioli al fiasco ✪✪

Dried haricot beans cooked traditionally – slowly in a flask. Originally, Chianti wine flasks were used; now corked glass flasks are sold specially for the purpose. The beans are served 'drowned' in olive oil as a vegetable. A Tuscan speciality.

Fagioli alla maruzzara ✪✪

Cannellini beans cooked in a tomato and oregano sauce. They are mixed with pasta to make a thick soup, typical of the Campania region (see recipe on page 106).

Fagioli all'uccelletto ✪✪✪

A Tuscan dish of cannellini beans cooked with garlic, sage and tomatoes, and served as a vegetable.

Fagioli con cotiche ✪✪

Cannellini beans, cooked in tomato sauce and flavoured with pork rind and fat from Parma ham. A typical Roman speciality that all true Romans have tasted at least once in their lives. A cast-iron digestion is needed here, but do try them!

Faraona alla creta ✪

A whole guinea fowl cooked in clay. This ancient way of cooking used by the Longobards to keep flavour and juices in, can still be found in Lombardy.

Farina

Flour.

Farinata ✪✪✪

A type of pancake made in Liguria from chick-pea flour, oilve oil and salt. It is baked in the oven until golden, then served piping

Crostini with parmesan curls

hot generously sprinkled with freshly ground black pepper.

Farsu magru, falso magro ✪✪✪

A tasty Sicilian stuffed meat roll. The filling, made from a minced beef and cheese mixture, is spread over a rectangle of veal, which is then garnished with sliced hard-boiled eggs, diced cheese and crumbled sausage. It is then rolled up, tied and braised slowly with chopped onion, tomatoes and wine.

Fave con pecorino ✪✪✪

Broad beans and pecorino cheese. On 1 May, the roads leading out of Rome are lined with stalls selling fresh broad beans, pecorino cheese and loaves of crusty bread, for the Romans to buy on their way to the traditional May Day picnic. This is, of course, accompanied by a bottle of wine from the Castelli.

Fegato

Liver.

Fegatelli di maiale ✪✪

Small pieces of pig's liver, seasoned and wrapped in caul fat with bay leaves, then fried in oil and wine. A tasty dish, traditionally served with PUNTARELLE (leafy salad vegetable).

Fegatini di pollo ✪

Chicken livers (or livers from other poultry). These can be sautéed in butter and served on croûtons, or made into a delicious pasta sauce called FINANZIERA.

Fegato alla veneziana ✪✪✪

Thin strips of calf's liver sautéed with onions and sprinkled with white wine. A famous dish that originated from Venice, which has become a national favourite (see recipe on page 110).

Fettuccine

Thin ribbons of freshly made pasta, usually served with a RAGÚ (meat) sauce.

Fichi ✪✪✪

Figs. Freshly picked figs, found in June and September are a real treat. Peel off the green skin and enjoy the sweet jam-like fruit inside. They are also dried in the sun, sometimes stuffed with almonds or baked, to make the dried figs (fichi secchi) eaten at Christmas.

Fichi d'India ✪✪✪

Prickly pears. They are found in the south

and Sardinia in late summer. These red, orange and yellow fruits must be treated with respect as their fine thorns can be very painful! Bought from street stalls, however, already peeled, they are quite safe. In Furore, on the Amalfi coast, there is a prickly pear festa on the first Sunday in September.

Finanziera, alla ✪✪✪

'Financier' style. A sauce made with chicken livers, onions and mushrooms cooked in white wine. In Piedmont, it incudes heart, kidneys and cock's combs, too.

Finocchio ✪✪✪

Fennel. This aniseed-flavoured vegetable is sliced and served in mixed salads, baked in the oven or simply served in wedges to be dipped in oil and salt to help the digestion after a rich meal. The rounder heads are referred to as 'male' (maschi) and they are more tender then the flatter ('female') heads.

Finocchiona ✪✪

A Tuscan salami made from minced pork, seasoned with fennel seeds. Look out for it hanging in the grocers' shops or, even better, ask the butcher if he makes his own. Umbria produces a similar salami called finocchiella.

Fior di latte ✪✪

A cheese, similar to mozzarella but made from cows' milk. A freshly made cheese, it has a rather rubbery texture and a fresh, milky flavour. It is best eaten the same day but it can be kept in the refrigerator if covered with its whey or with milk.

Fiori di zucchini ✪✪✪

Courgette flowers. Delicious coated in a light batter and fried. They can be stuffed with mozzarella and anchovy fillets, but are good just on their own. If you decide to experiment, open them up under running water, to make sure there are no insects inside, then pat dry before coating with batter.

42

A selection of cheeses from the Alpine regions of Piedmont

Focaccia ✪

Very similar to pizza, but more bread-like. Usually served split in half and filled with cheese and/or salami.

Fonduta alla valdostana ✪✪✪

A traditional cheese dip from Valle d'Aosta. It is made from FONTINA cheese, milk, butter and egg yolks and is served in special terracotta bowls, over burners that keep it hot, with cubes of toasted bread. Very rich and filling, but not to be missed.

Fontina ✪

A cheese made from cows' milk, produced solely in the Valle d'Aosta. The large, round, flat cheeses are salted and matured in special grottos, and only those considered perfect are stamped with the official Fontina seal. The cheese is golden yellow with a compact texture and a mild flavour that becomes stronger as it matures.

Formaggio

Cheese.

Fragoline ✪✪✪

Tiny wild strawberries with a strongly scented flavour. Often sold in baskets at the roadside, they tend to be quite expensive. Only rinse them very gently before serving or they will disintegrate!

Frappè ✪✪

Thin strips of fried dough-like pastry,

dredged with icing sugar. Mountains of these pastries can be seen in bars and cake shops at *carnevale* time (before Lent). They are so light that an *etto* (100g/4oz) goes a long way!

Frattaglie

Offal.

Freselle ✪

Large crisp rings of biscuity bread. Used instead of croûtons or as the basis of a summer snack, *panzanella* (see recipe on page 114).

Friarielli ✪✪✪

The very tips and flowers of BROCCOLETTI. In Naples, they are fried in oil and garlic and served with sausages. Very bitter tasting.

Frittata ✪✪

The Italian answer to the Spanish *tortilla*. The 'filling', such as courgettes, onions or artichokes, is first chopped and cooked in the pan. Then seasoned beaten egg and grated cheese are added. It is browned on both sides and served in slices (see recipe on page 112).

Frittata con erbe ✪✪

Frittata with herbs. Traditionally made from at least seven different herbs or greens

43

picked in the fields. A dish from Friuli, it is usually made from spinach, beet tops, leeks, thyme, sage, basil and parsley. They are first boiled, then fried in oil, garlic and chopped onion before the egg is added.

Fritto misto all'italiana ✪✪✪

A mixed fry. This platter of crisp golden morsels varies from region to region, but the most common constituents are mozzarella balls, potato croquettes, brains, tiny lamb cutlets, courgettes, artichokes, aubergine wedges and cauliflower florets, all dipped in batter and deep fried.

Frittura di paranza ✪✪✪

The smaller, less important fish in the catch, from the local offshore fishing boats, fried and served with wedges of lemon. They are usually so fresh (these less prized fish do not keep), that they taste and smell of the sea!

Frittura di pesce ✪✪✪

Small fish mixed with rings of squid and a few prawns, all dipped in thin batter and fried until crisp and golden. Ask for just the squid and prawns if you cannot cope with the heads and bones of the whole fish.

Wild mushurooms, one of Piedmont's gastronomic delights

Frutti di bosco ✪

'Woodland fruits'. This mixture of wild strawberries, raspberries, blackberries, bilberries and redcurrents is served with sugar and lemon juice or topped with freshly whipped cream and ice-cream.

Frutti di mare ✪✪✪

Zoologically speaking, shellfish such as clams, mussels, scallops, razor shells and oysters. When ordering *spaghetti con frutti di mare*, however, do not be surprised if a few prawns and squid have crept in, too.

Funghi

Mushrooms. There are many different types of edible mushrooms but they all have specific names by which they are known, except for the cultivated *champignons*, which are called simply *funghi*.

Funghi trifolati ✪✪

Sliced mushrooms sautéed in butter and garlic. They are served warm sprinkled with chopped parsley.

Fusilli

Pasta sprials that can be short or as long as spaghetti.

G

Gamberi, gamberoni ✪✪
Prawns and giant prawns. They are served whole, fried with rings of squid, or grilled, or cooked with tomatoes to make a pasta sauce.

Gelato
Ice-cream (see box above).

Genovese, alla ✪✪✪
This meat and onion sauce is an old Neapolitan recipe. Served with short pasta and lots of grated Parmesan.

Genovese, la ✪✪✪
A joint of beef cooked with twice its weight of onions. The onions cook down to make the delicious sauce served with pasta, while the meat is sliced and served with chipped potatoes. Despite its name, it is an ancient Neapolitan recipe.

Ghiotta, alla
A way of grilling or roasting meat or fish on the spit. It is basted with a sauce made from the fish or meat juices, mixed with olive oil, wine or vinegar, chopped ham or bacon, capers, olives, crushed anchovy fillets, garlic and cloves, all cooked in the drip tray below. This drip tray, called *leccarda*, gives its name to the dish, too.

Gnocchetti sardi or malloreddus ✪✪✪
Typical Sardinian pasta in the shape of tiny GNOCCHI, which look rather like shells. Served with a spicy tomato sauce.

Gnocchi ✪✪✪
Unless specified otherwise, tiny cushions or rolls of very lights dough made from potatoes and flour. They are cooked in boiling water and served with a tomato or meat sauce, with grated Parmesan. In the Roman *trattorie*, the set day for eating gnocchi is Thursday. Green gnocchi, mixed with spinach (*spinaci*) or nettle (*ortica*), are served with a butter or cream sauce.

Gnocchi alla romana ✪
Roman-style gnocchi. Semolina rounds layered with butter and cheese, then baked in the oven until golden.

Cooling off with an ice-cream

45

GRANA – HARD CHEESE WITH A POWERFUL FLAVOUR

Parmesan must be the best known of these hard cheeses produced on the Padua Plain; however, the fresh cheese bears no resemblance to the dry and dusty contents of the small tubs lurking on the supermarket shelves back home. A chunk of fresh *grana* has a certain sweetness combined with its heady flavour and aroma. They are made from partially skimmed cows' milk and have a granular texture which gives them their name. Depending on the geographical region of production, they are called *parmigiano-reggiano*, *lodigiano*, *grana padano*, or just *grana*. The enormous round cheese are broken open, never cut. It is fascinating to watch a grocer at work while opening a new cheese. A special pointed knife acts as a lever to split the cheese in two and then into portions.

Gorgonzola ☻
Famous, creamy blue cheese made from cows' milk. It is produced in Lombardy near the town that gave it its name many years ago (and where it was originally produced by mistake!). The cheeses, weighing 10kg/22lb each, are left to mature and form the characteristic dark green mould that gives the strong flavour. Mild Gorgonzola is also sometimes layered with creamy MASCARPONE. It is delicious, but very fattening!

Grana ☻☻☻
The generic name for the hard cheeses (see box above). Some are better known as Parmesan.

Granchio ☻
Crab. Particularly popular in Sardinia, where crabs are cooked in tomato sauce and served with spaghetti. You have to be an expert spaghetti eater to cope with the bits of shell that get in the way. Not for beginners!

Granoturco ☻
Corn on the cob. In the south it is barbecued on the spit and sold by the roadside.

Granseola ☻
A large crab. Found along the Adriatic coast from Venice to Trieste, it is served dressed, in its shell.

Gnocchi, *a Roman speciality*

Grigliata mista ✿✿

Mixed grill. A firm favourite in country *trattorie* where an open wood fire is used for grilling meats. A standard mixed grill includes lamb cutlets, pork chops, quail, sausages and chicken, with variations such as rabbit, spare ribs of pork and suckling pig.

Grissini

Breadsticks. Turin is the home of breadsticks, which were originally made by hand all over Piedmont. Now made industrially, they are exported all over the world. In Turin you can still buy home-made ones in some bakeries, where you are spoilt for choice by those flavoured or enriched with spices, seed, oil, butter and malt. Wholemeal flour may also be used.

Gubana ✿

Sweet bread roll, filled with dried fruits, candied peel and nuts. This delicious bread comes from Fruili.

Gulasch ✿✿

Hot, spicy meat dish, made from beef, onions and paprika. Found in the mountainous regions of Alto Adige and Fruili, it is served with boiled potatoes or POLENTA.

I

Impepata di cozze, 'mpepata di cozze ✿✿✿

Mussels cooked in their own juice with the addition of chopped parsley and lashings of freshly ground pepper. Not to be missed when on the coast around Naples or further south (see recipe on page 105).

In bianco

Plain, without sauce. On menus, *pesce in bianco* is poached fish, which you then dress to your liking. Italians say they are eating *in bianco* when not feeling too well. They dress their pasta with olive oil or butter and grated Parmesan, have their meat or fish poached or grilled, and eat their vegetables boiled.

In carpione

Usually means pickled in vinegar, wine and lemon juice after being seasoned with a mixture of herbs and spices. In Lombardy the game or fish is then served with its jelly-like sauce.

In porchetta

Roast-pork style. Game or poultry is stuffed with a mixture of chopped liver, bacon or ham, rosemary, garlic and fennel, browned in olive oil and cooked with wine until tender.

Indivia ✿✿

A bitter-tasting leafy salad vegetable with thin, curly, spiky leaves, yellowish green in the centre, becoming darker towards the outside. It is also known as *insalata riccia* (curly salad). Displayed in the market stall, they look like curly wigs!

Insaccati

Dried sausages. Meaning 'in the sack', they include salami, and are made from spiced minced or chopped pork that is forced into different shaped 'sacks' made from natural fibres. The sausages are then salted and hung to mature in a cool, dry place.

Insalata caprese ✿✿

A summer salad of mozzarella cheese, tomatoes and fresh basil. Originally from Capri, it is now a national favourite (see recipe on page 114).

Insalata di mare ✿✿✿

A seafood salad, including diced octopus, squid, prawns, clams and mussels, mixed with chopped celery and garlic, then dressed with olive oil and lemon juice. Delicious when chilled and served as a starter or summer main course.

Insalata di riso ✿✿

Cold rice salad. Often found in bars or *tavole calde*. Chilled boiled rice is mixed with various savoury ingredients and dressed with oil and lemon or mayonnaise (see recipe on page 114).

Insalata mista ✿

Mixed salad served as a side course. It usually lives up to its name and includes anything the chef decides to put in it.

Insalata verde ✿

Green salad. An Italian green salad can be an unforgettable experience if you are lucky enough to find a country *trattoria* which serves a mixture of freshly picked leaves. You will probably have fun guessing what each one is! It is served with oil and vinegar, so if you prefer it plain tell the waiter not to dress it – *'Senza condimento, per favore'*.

Involtini ✿

Stuffed meat rolls. When made from slices of beef these are similar to beef olives (rolled, stuffed, thinly sliced beef). Flavoured with garlic and parsley or carrot and celery,

Mozzarella and tomato salad

they are served in tomato sauce. Watch out for the cocktail stick used to secure the rolls of meat.

J

Jota ✪✪
A thick soup from Friuli. Made from beans, sauerkraut and maizemeal, it is flavoured with lard, onion, sage, parsley and garlic. When meat or salami is added, it becomes a substantial one-course meal.

L

Lamponi
Raspberries. Best in summer.

Lasagne ✪✪✪
There are several regional recipes for this well-known baked pasta dish. The classic lasagne comes from Emilia-Romagna where the strips of green or white pasta are layered with BOLOGNESE sauce, white sauce and Parmesan cheese.

Lasagne alla napoletana ✪✪✪
Neapolitan Lasagne strips are longer and thinner and layered with RAGÙ sauce, tiny meat balls, smoke mozzarella, sliced hard-boiled eggs, salami and ricotta cheese. The ends of the strips fold over to seal the top, which is then garnished with more meat balls and diced cheese, sprinkled with Parmesan and baked until golden. Can be found on Sundays and holidays, especially around *carnevale* time (before Lent).

Latterini ✪✪
Tiny poached fish dressed with oil and lemon juice. A real delicacy for fish lovers.

Lattuga
Lettuce.

Lauro
Bay leaves. Used to flavour soups, stews, roast meat and liver. Fresh leaves can be picked from the bushes in parks and gardens.

Lenticchie ✪✪
Lentils. Cooked either with ham, or garlic, tomatoes and parsley, they are served as a vegetable or a thick pasta soup. Lentils are traditionally eaten on New Year's Eve to bring wealth as they symbolise 'money'.

Lenticchie alla montanara ✪✪
Lentil and chestnut soup from Abruzzo. Flavoured with bay leaves, marjoram and basil. It is served with thick slices of toasted bread.

Lasagne, one of Italy's most popular dishes

Good fresh seafood forms the basis for Venetian cuisine

Lepre in salmì ✪✪
A very rich jugged hare. The hare is marinated and cooked in red wine with a mixture of spices. Found in Lombardy, Piedmont and Trentino, it is traditionally served with POLENTA.

Limoni
Lemons. Freshly picked lemons, with their dark green leaves, can be found on market stalls in the south. Some will have come from Amalfi, famous for its lemon groves. The very large lemons grown on Procida, one of the smaller islands in the Bay of Naples, are sliced, sprinkled with sugar and eaten as a dessert.

Linguine
This flat SPAGHETTI is traditionally served with 'pesto' sauce in Genoa.

Lombata di maiale ✪
A simple pork chop, either grilled over a wood or charcoal fire or fried in olive oil with garlic and fennel seeds.

Lonza ✪✪
Like a very fatty ham or a very lean salami: it is half-way between the two. In late autumn and winter, after the pigs have been slaughtered, you can see the freshly cured *lonze*, parcelled up in brown paper and string, hanging in country butchers' shops. They have to mature in a cool, dry place before being opened and sliced.

Luccio
Pike.

Lumache ✪✪
Snails. The ancient Romans bred snails along their moss-covered city walls. Still served in Rome, they are cooked in a spicy green sauce on the eve of St John's Day. Legend has it that on this day, witches and devils surround St John's Basilica where the skull of the saint is kept. To protect themselves, the Romans used to ring the church bells, hang strings of garlic behind their doors, and eat snails, which symbolise the devil. The more snails they managed to eat the better!

M

Maccheroni alla chitarra ✪✪
Freshly made pasta from Abruzzo that looks like 'square' spaghetti. It was originally made by pressing the rolled pasta dough through the strings of a *chitarra* (a series of wires stretched over a wooden frame, similar to a guitar). It is traditionally served with a chilli sauce or a rich RAGÙ, made from lamb, tomatoes, peppers and chillies.

Macedonia di frutta ✪

Fresh fruit salad. This varies with the season, but can always be found on menus, dressed with sugar and lemon juice, or sometimes a sweet liqueur.

Mafaldine

These frilly ribbons of pasta are named after the trimmings on Princess Mafalda's dresses. They are traditionally served in the south with RAGÚ (meat) sauce.

Maiale

Pork.

Malloreddus

See GNOCCHETTI SARDI.

Mandaranci

Mandarins. Best in wintertime.

Mandarini

Tangerines. Best in wintertime.

Mandorle

Almonds. In the southern regions of Apulia, Calabria and Sicily, the pink and white almond blossom appears soon after Christmas. Almonds are used extensively in the production of sweets, cakes and liqueurs, not to mention the almond nougat made in Cremona that is exported all over the world.

Manzo

Beef.

Margarina

Margarine.

Maritozzi con la panna ✪

Sweet bread buns split in half and filled to overflowing with freshly whipped cream. Can be found in most Roman bars.

Marmellata

Jam.

Marrons glacés ✪✪✪

Large, succulent, candied chestnuts. Unfortunately, they are only available during the winter, sold loose in cake shops and boxed for giving away at Christmas.

Mascarpone ✪

A cream cheese. Although classed as cheese, it tastes more like clotted cream. Delicious spread on bread or served with strawberries, it is sold loose in the grocer's and pre-packed in supermarkets.

Mazzancolle ✪✪✪

Giant prawns, also called GAMBERONI. They are grilled on skewers over a wood or charcoal fire. Six or eight are a normal portion, so don't order them as your main course if you are really hungry!

Melanzane

Aubergines. These are a summer vegetable which can be found all year round; the most common are the shiny, oblong, dark purple ones. Choose those which are firm to touch and not too large, to avoid finding them full of seeds.

Melanzane al funghetto ✪✪

Diced aubergines, fried in olive oil and garlic with a little tomato and fresh basil. It is served as a vegetable in the south.

Melanzane alla parmigiana ✪✪✪

A favourite summer dish made from fried aubergines layered with tomato sauce, mozzarella and grated Parmesan, then baked in the oven (see recipe on page 111).

Mele

Apples.

Melone

Melon.

Merluzzo

Cod.

Mesciuà ✪✪

A bean, sweetcorn and chick-pea soup from Liguria.

Mezzafegato ✪

Unusual raw sausages made from pigs' livers mixed with sugar, pepper, sultanas, pine kernels and orange peel. Grilled and served hot, they are not to everyone's taste.

Mimosa ✪

A gateau, made from sponge cake and whipped cream. It is decorated with bright yellow cake crumbs to resemble the strongly scented mimosa flowers found all over the countryside in springtime.

Minestra maritata ✪✪

A Neapolitan dish made from green leafy vegetables, such as chard or sprouting broccoli, cooked with cheese and served in a meat broth, made by boiling offcuts of pork with sausages and salami.

Minestrone ✪✪

A thick soup originating in 11th-century

Walnuts, grown in Sorrento

Lombardy. Vegetables, beans and salted meats were cooked together in a large cauldron and eaten as a ritual food to bring rain. Nowadays, cured ham or bacon replace the salted meats, and the vegetables vary from season to season, but minestrone is still basically a thick soup. Pasta or rice is often cooked in it before it is served with grated Parmesan (see recipe on page 102).

Minestrone di orzo e fagioli ✪✪
Thick soup made from beans and pearl barley. A regional speciality from Friuli, it is flavoured with chopped ham rind and lard.

Missultitt ✪✪✪
A dish made from salted, dried fish. Found around Lake Como, it consists of salted fish, dried in the sun, then grilled and served with oil and vinegar. Delicious, but makes you rather thirsty.

Misticanza ✪✪✪
A selection of mixed green leaves, usually picked wild in the countryside, served as a salad. The overall flavour can be rather bitter, so keep to lettuce unless you are adventurous.

Monte Bianco ✪✪✪
Mont Blanc. Deliciously sweet cake made by piling whipped cream and meringues on to a flaky pastry base, then covering them with piped chestnut paste to look like Europe's highest mountain, Mont Blanc. Not to be missed if you have a sweet tooth.

More
Blackberries. Best in summer.

Mortadella ✪✪
The Italian answer to luncheon meat. It has a slightly stronger flavour and contains peppercorns and pistachio nuts. Delicious sliced thinly and eaten as a filling in a crispy roll; it is quite cheap too.

Mostarda ✪✪
A mixture of fruit pickled in a mustard sauce from Cremona. Excellent with boiled meats.

Mozzarella ✪✪✪
A semi-soft cheese. Originally it was made from buffalos' milk in Campania and southern Lazio, where water buffalos are still bred. Nowadays, it is also made from a mixture of buffalos' and cows' milk, but the real mozzarella still comes from its region of origin. The cheese is moulded into spherical shapes with a knot on the top, or into plaits and bite-sized portions called *bocconcini*. Whatever their shape, they must all be kept in their whey or, like the tiny mozzarellas made near Salerno, buried in thick cream!

Mozzarella in carrozza ✪✪
Crisp, golden mozzarella 'sandwiches' dipped in egg and fried until golden. A typical Neapolitan dish meaning 'mozzarella in the coach', it makes a pleasant alternative to meat or fish (see recipe on page 112).

N

Nervetti or nervitt ✪✪
Calf's foot boiled with vegetables, then served cold, cut into slivers, with raw, sliced onion, black pepper, parsley and olive oil. Borlotti beans can be added if liked. This is a typical dish from Lombardy.

Nocciole
Hazelnuts. These are grown in parts of northern, central and southern Italy, and in late August and September you can see piles of them left to dry in the sun. Try the fresh hazelnuts on sale at the greengrocer's. Dried, they are used to make cakes, chocolates and chocolate spread.

Noci
Walnuts. Sorrento is famous for its walnuts, which have large, smooth, pale brown shells. In their natural state they are quite dark but are washed to make them look more appetising! Apart from being served as a dessert, they are used to make liqueurs, and chopped and mixed with cream to make a delicious pasta sauce.

Norcina, alla ✪✪✪
Sauce made with crumbled sausages, onion and chillies mixed with cream. Traditionally

served with RIGATONI and lots of grated Parmesan.

Norma, alla ✪✪✪

Named after Bellini's famous opera, this sauce is made from aubergines, tomatoes and basil. A Sicilian speciality.

O

Olio d'olive

Olive oil. The main regions producing olive oil are Liguria, Tuscany and Apulia. The quality of the oil depends on the quality of the olives and how they are harvested; they must not be damaged in any way or the oil will be too acidic. The best oils are expensive because the oilves are hand picked. *Olio extra vergine d'oliva* (extra fine olive oil) comes from the first pressings and is the best for dressings. The farm-produced olive oils are the most genuine and can be bought direct from the farm. This oil has often not been filtered and looks rather cloudy, but has a rich, dark yellowy-green colour. It is excellent simply on crusty bread sprinkled with salt.

Olive

Olives. The small black olives from Gaeta are used for making sauces or seasoned with orange peel and fennel seeds, then served with starters. Large green sweet-tasting olives are sold in paper cones by the roadside. There are smaller, green, bitter

Olives, a major contribution to the local diet

tasting olives dressed with garlic, chillies and oregano. Then, there are the stuffed olives you find in your Martini and fried olives from Ascoli Piceno. A selection of small, plump, black or green types can usually be found in all good grocers, where they are sold loose, so you can ask for a mixture and try them all! (See box below.)

Olive ascolane ✪✪✪

Large, green olives from Ascoli Piceno, stuffed with a minced meat mixture, dipped in egg and breadcrumbs and fried. In the Marches, they can be found in the FRITTO MISTO.

Orecchiette ✪✪✪

'Little ears' of pasta. Still made by hand from an old recipe. In Apulia, their place of origin, they are traditionally served with a sauce

---

ANCIENT TREES BEARING VERSATILE FRUIT

The gnarled appearance of many olive trees matches their longevity, for they are expected to live for anything up to 600 to 700 years and there are tales of trees far older.

The fruit-bearing pattern tends to be a good harvest once every two years. Green olives are harvested around September or October. Black olives are the ripened fruit and they are ready for picking from November to December. Fruit destined for oil production is harvested around January.

The method of harvesting may be as important as the quality of the crop, as only hand-picked olives are used to make the finest oils. Mechanical picking involves shaking the olives from the trees.

Freshly picked olives are bitter and the traditional treatment involves soaking the fruit in regular changes of water or brine for up to 15 days. Only then are they ready for pickling in brine or flavouring with herbs and spices, and combining with oil.

The ripened, perfect fruit are pressed to yield their oil – the best, dark and thick, is the first to come from the fruit. This is not acidic but as the fruit is pressed again the oil has a higher acidic content and a less pronounced, smooth flavour. Finally, the cheapest, lightest and most acidic of the oils is extracated from the remains of the fruit. Oil from the final pressings has to be purified, sometimes balanced by the addition of an alkali.

made from turnip tops (*come di rape*) but can also be dressed with a rich RAGÚ.

Origano
Oregano. This herb is found growing wild and is hung in bunches to dry under the arched porchways. It is used generously in many dishes.

Ossobuco alla milanese ✪✪✪
Thick marrow-bone veal steaks, cooked in butter and wine with *gremolada*, a mixture of finely chopped garlic, lemon peel and rosemary. A special spoon is used for eating the marrow, which is considered a delicacy. A traditional Milanese dish that has become a national favourite, but is often found cooked in tomato sauce nowadays.

P

Pagliata ✪✪✪
Pajata, in Roman dialect, this is the milk-filled intestines of a suckling calf, cooked in a spicy tomato sauce and served with *rigatoni*. This delicacy can be found in the *osterie* in Testaccio, and old part of Rome near the slaughterhouse.

Pancetta
Bacon.

Pandoro ✪
A large, tall, star-shaped cake, similar to rum baba in texture, dredged with icing sugar. Served at Christmas, it was originally made in Verona but has become a national favourite.

Pane
Bread.

Panettone ✪
A light, sweet sultana bread which for centuries has been eaten at Christmas. Legend has it that in the 15th century, in the days of Ludovico il Moro, a baker's boy wanting to ingratiate himself with his master, Toni (he wished to marry his daughter!), gave him a special cake recipe. This proved to be a great success when sold as *Pan di Toni*. The name has since been transformed into *panettone* – literally 'large bread'.

Panforte ✪✪
Another Christmas speciality, this time from Siena. It is made from candied peel, sultanas and nuts, spiced and packed together so tightly that the cake is difficult to cut but delicious to eat!

Paniscia ✪✪
A warming, thick soup made from rice, lard, sausage, cabbage and beans. Served in winter in Valle d'Aosta.

Pappa col pomodoro ✪✪✪
A thick Tuscan bread soup with tomatoes and basil. Eaten hot or cold.

Pappardelle ✪✪✪
Wide, ribbon-shaped pasta. Traditionally served with rich meat sauces such as hare – *pappardelle al sugo di lepre* is a dish found in Tuscany.

Parmigiano ✪✪✪
Parmesan. Probably the most famous Italian cheese. It is the regional name for a type of GRANA.

Passatelli di carne ✪✪✪
Freshly made noodles from a mixture of minced chicken, spinach and breadcrumbs, seasoned with nutmeg. They are served in consumeé. A regional dish from The Marches.

Passato di . . .
Vegetables or tomatoes turned into purée, either in a blender or by passing them through a sieve.

Pasta
This can be traced back to Sicily in the Middle Ages. It is now industrially made from durum wheat ground into semolina, mixed with water and forced through nozzles to make different pasta shapes (see box on page 56).

Pasta al forno
Baked pasta. The pasta is mixed with sauce, layered with other ingredients and baked in the oven. The most famous is LASAGNE, but there are also other variations such as RIGATONI mixed with white sauce, chopped ham, mushrooms and peas and sprinkled with breadcrumbs and grated cheese (see recipe on page 105).

Pasta asciutta
Pasta served with a sauce.

Pasta con le sarde ✪✪✪
A traditional sardine dish from Sicily. Sardines are layered with pasta, coated with a sauce made from sardines, anchovies, chopped onion, sultanas, pine kernels, the local wild fennel and saffron, then baked in

Colourful display of dried pasta found in Pasta Fresca *shops*

MANY SHAPES, SIZES AND COLOURS

There is an enormous variety of dried pasta shapes available and new ones are always being manufactured. Spinach, tomato and saffron are just three ingredients which may be used to colour and flavour the dough. Names may change from region to region but most shapes are made both smooth (*liscia*) or ribbed (*rigata*). Some of the more common dried pasta shapes are listed alphabetically in this section.

Pasta should always be cooked by dropping it into plenty of fast-boiling salted water. Test it two or three minutes before the end of the recommended cooking time. It is perfectly cooked when the uncooked core in the centre is just about to disappear or, in the case of spaghetti, when you can squeeze it between your thumb and forefinger to break it. This state is called *al dente* which means 'resistant to the tooth'. Drain the pasta immediately and mix with the sauce. (If not using a tomato-based sauce, keep a little of the pasta water for mixing, if liquid is needed.)

the oven. An unusual mixture which is very tasty and not to be missed when in Sicily.

Pasta e . . .
Usually refers to short pasta shapes, cooked or mixed with vegetables or pulses. They are sometimes referred to as 'thick pasta soups' or *minestre*. Some of the more common are mentioned below.

Pasta e cavolfiori ✪✪✪
With cauliflower, olives and capers.

Pasta e ceci ✪✪✪
With chick-peas and rosemary.

Pasta e fagioli ✪✪✪
With beans, the recipe varying from region to region (see recipe on page 106).

Pasta e lenticchie ✪✪✪
With lentils, often flavoured with ham.

Pasta e patate ✪✪✪
With potatoes, often flavoured with celery.

Pasta e piselli ✪✪✪
With peas flavoured with onions and ham (see recipe on page 110).

Pasta e zucca ✪✪✪
With highly peppered pumpkin.

Pasta fresca ✪✪✪
Fresh pasta. It is easier than you think to make fresh pasta from flour and eggs. When in Italy, take advantage of the *Pasta Fresca* shops and choose from the many shapes and colours produced. The most

Pasta quills in tomato sauce

common are the ribbon-shaped ones starting with the wide *lasagne*, then *pappardelle*, *fettuccine*, *tagliatelle*, down to the fine *tagliolini*. You can also find fresh coloured pasta – green with spinach, red with tomato and brown with mushroom or truffle. There are also stuffed fresh pastas such as TORTELLINI, RAVIOLI, AGNOLOTTI and CANNELLONI.

Pasta 'ncasciata ✪✪✪
A Sicilian savoury baked dish. A tin is lined with aubergines and hard-boiled eggs, then filled with pasta mixed with tomato and basil sauce, chopped salami, diced mozzarella and grated Parmesan. It is baked until golden, then turned out on to a serving dish and sprinkled generously with more grated Parmesan.

Paste reali
Literally 'royal cakes'. Marzipan is rolled and cut into different shapes, iced and decorated with silver balls. Found in Naples and the south at Christmas.

Pasticcio di maccheroni ✪✪
A sweet short-crust pie filled with pasta coated with a rich meat sauce, from Emilia-Romagna. A sweet-sour combination served hot or cold.

Pastiera napoletana ✪✪✪
A sweet pastry case filled with sweetened ricotta cheese, egg yolks, candied peel and sweetcorn. It is traditionally served at Easter in Naples and the south. For cheesecake fans.

Patate
Potatoes.

Pecorino ✪✪✪
A hard cheese, made from ewes' milk, found particularly in Lazio, Tuscany, Sicily and Sardinia. Look out for the locally made cheeses sold on market stalls or by the roadside. *Pecorino* has a strong, sharp flavour, is delicious with olives and is frequently served grated with pasta.

Penne
Pasta quills.

Pepe
Pepper.

Peperonata ✪✪
Red and yellow peppers fried in olive oil and garlic with onions and tomatoes. Served as a vegetable, it is a delicious (but often highly indigestible) dish.

Peperoncino
Dried red chillies. They are used extensively, both ground and whole. Dried and threaded on string, they look attractive hung in the kitchen.

Peperoni ripieni or imbottiti ✪
Stuffed peppers. They make a delicious main course in the summer. The filling varies from region to region and can be based on minced meat, tuna or other vegetables such as aubergines. Served hot or cold.

Peperoni
Peppers.

Pere
Pears.

Pernice
Partridge.

Pescatora, alla
Fisherman's sauce. It contains seafood and shellfish, and is served with tomatoes or without (IN BIANCO). Often spiced with chilli.

Pesce
Fish.

Pesce arrosto ✪✪✪
A whole fish 'roasted' or baked in the oven with a little garlic, parsley, olive oil and wine. It is filleted and 'beheaded' by the waiter. Be careful when ordering it, as the price quoted on menus usually refers to 100g/4oz – the fish is sold by weight, and is usually meant to be eaten by at least two people, depending on size.

Pesce persico ✪✪
Perch. When made into a risotto, it is a speciality of the lakeside restaurants around Lake Como.

Pesce spada
Swordfish. These huge fish, with their long pointed 'swords' and their silvery skins, can be seen on the fishmongers' slabs, where they are cut into steaks, ready to be baked or barbecued. A real treat, and no bones to cope with!

Pesce spada alla ghiotta ✪✪
Swordfish cooked in a rich tomato sauce flavoured with capers and black olives, from Messina.

Nectarines, a taste of summer

Pesce spada alla griglia ✪✪✪
Baked or barbecued swordfish.

Pesche
Peaches. Best in summer.

Pesto genovese ✪✪✪
Famous basil sauce from Genoa. Fresh basil leaves, garlic, pine kernels and grated percorino cheese are chopped and pounded together in a pestile and mortar. Then olive oil is slowly added to make a smooth green paste. It is served with pasta or used to flavour minestrone. Some people now use a blender, but not without feeling guilty (see recipe on page 107).

Peverada ✪
A strong-tasting sauce made from chicken livers, anchovy fillets, pickles, parsley and grated cheese, mixed with vinegar and cooked with garlic-flavoured olive oil. Served with poultry in Veneto.

Pezzenta ✪
Once a tasty 'poor man's' salami, made from pork offcuts highly seasoned with pepper and garlic. Now it is enjoyed by rich and poor alike!

Piadina romagnola ✪✪
Thin, pizza-like rounds of bread. Found in bars and on roadside stalls, they are heated up, filled with Parma ham and cheese, then folded in half. An excellent snack when touring Romagna.

Piccante
Food spiced with chilli or, in the case of cheese, with a strong flavour.

Piccatina al limone ✪
Thin veal escalopes cooked in butter and lemon juice, and sprinkled with chopped parsley. A dish with a really fresh flavour.

Pinolata ✪
A type of Madeira cake flavoured with pine kernels. Cut into slices and served with Vin Santo (sweet wine) as a dessert in Tuscany.

Pinoli
Pine kernels. They are found in the cones of the Mediterranean cluster-pines which abound in central and southern Italy. Also sold ready-shelled in small packets, or loose from the grocer's, they are an essential ingredient in PESTO. Expensive, but 100g/4oz go a long way, and they keep well in an airtight jar.

Pinzimonio or cazzimperia ✪
A dip made from olive oil, salt and freshly ground black pepper. A selection of raw vegetables, such as celery, spring onions, carrots, radishes and fennel are used for dippers. Deliciously refreshing after a rich meal.

Piselli al prosciutto ✪✪
Peas cooked with chopped onion and ham (see recipe on page 110).

Pitta ✪
Calabrian name for pizza-pie. It is usually filled with ricotta, sausage and hard-boiled eggs or tuna, tomatoes, black olives and capers. Made from recipes handed down from mother to daughter, pitta is rarely found outside the home.

Pizza
Pizzas, as we know them today, originated in Naples in the 18th century. Neapolitan pizza has a high border and is slightly thicker than the Roman variety. But whatever its origin, a genuine pizza must be cooked in a wood-fired oven, next to the glowing embers (see box on page 60).

Pizza di Pasqua
A cheese-flavoured bread made with ewes' milk cheese. Originally made only at Easter, it can now be found all year round in Umbria.

Pizzaiola, alla ✪✪
Pizza-maker's sauce. Made from slices of beef cooked with tomatoes, garlic and oregano. The meat is then served as the main course (see recipe on page 109).

Pizzelle ✪✪✪
Small, fried pizzas. Topped with tomato and

Pizza ai funghi and mozzarella

TRADITIONAL PIZZA TOPPINGS

✪✪ **Pizza ai Funghi** with tomatoes, mozzarella and sliced mushrooms.

✪✪ **Pizza alla Pescatora** with seafood and tomatoes.

✪✪ **Pizza Bianca** with olive oil and sea salt. Often served as bread in restaurants.

✪✪✪ **Pizza Capricciosa or Quattro Stagioni** with mixed ingredients such as tomatoes, mozzarella, ham, mushrooms, pickles, olives and anchovy fillets. Something to suit all 'four seasons' and to satisfy even the most 'capricious' customer!

✪✪✪ **Pizza Magherita** was first made by Raffaele Esposito, a Neapolitan *pizzaiuolo* in honour of Queen Magherita. He topped it all with the Italian colours of red

(tomatoes), white (mozzarella) and green (basil).

✪✪ **Pizza Marinara** with black olives, capers, anchovies and tomatoes.

✪✪✪ **Pizza Napoletana** is the name given in Rome to the topping made from tomatoes, mozzarella and anchovy fillets.

✪✪✪ **Pizza Romana** is the name given in Naples to the *pizza napoletana* served in Rome!

✪✪ **Pizza e Taglio** is the favourite Italian take-away. This pizza, sold by the slice, and topped with the usual toppings plus many more, is wrapped in paper and eaten in the street or parcelled up to take home.

basil and sprinkled with Parmesan, they are a Neopolitan favourite. They can also be dipped in sugar to make a sweet (see recipe on page 113).

Pizzoccheri   ✪✪✪
Ribbon-shaped pasta made from white and buckwheat flour. From the Valtellina, it is cooked with cabbage and potatoes and layered with slices of BITTO cheese and grated Parmesan. Coated with melted garlic butter before serving, it makes a delicious one-course meal.

Polenta   ✪✪✪
Made from maize flour and water, polenta is like a very thick savoury semolina. It is left to cool and cut into slices, then baked or fried. Polenta is served in this way in the north, with game and fish cooked in sauces, as a main course. In central and southern Italy, a more fluid version is served on special wooden plates. The polenta is topped with meat and tomato sauce made with sausages or spare-ribs or pork and sprinkled with grated pecorino cheese. Served as a first course, this also makes a filling one-course meal.

Polenta 'grasa'   ✪✪✪
Cubes of FONTINA cheese and butter mixed with polenta. When this dish from the Valle d'Aosta is served, everyone helps themselves from the pan placed in the centre of the table.

Pollo
Chicken.

Pollo alla Marengo   ✪✪
Chicken pieces served in a wine sauce, topped with croûtons, eggs and prawns. Originally, it was a simple chicken dish offered to Napoleon at an inn in Marengo, after his victory over the Austrians.

Pollo alla romana   ✪✪
Roman style chicken. Cooked with tomatoes, peppers, garlic and wine.

Pollo arrosto   ✪✪
Freshly barbecued chicken with crisp golden skin, beautifully seasoned. It can be bought in the *rosticceria* and *pizza a taglio* shops. With roast potatoes, it makes a delicious ready-made meal.

Polpette   ✪
Meatballs made from minced beef, flavoured with cheese, parsley and onion or garlic. They can either be fried and served as a main course or cooked in tomato sauce. A sweet-sour version can be found in the south, made from minced pork, pine kernels and sultanas.

Polpettone   ✪
A meat loaf very similar to the POLPETTE.

Polpi affogati   ✪✪✪
Octopuses which have been 'drowned' in a spicy tomato sauce. This Neapolitan speciality is delicious with spaghetti (see recipe on page 106).

Polpo

Octopus.

Polpo all'insalata ✪✪

A chilled salad made from boiled octopus chopped into small pieces and mixed with garlic, celery, carrot and parsley. It is dressed with olive oil and lemon juice. Served as a starter or summer main dish, this salad is a 'must' for adventurous fish lovers.

Pomodori

Tomatoes. These grow in all shapes and sizes. The small cherry tomato is hung under porchways to provide 'fresh' tomatoes for winter sauces. The plum-shaped San Marzano tomato is canned and exported all over the world. The strange-looking ribbed tomato is ideal for salads or, when too ripe, for stuffing and baking in the oven.

Pomodori con riso ✪✪✪

Tomatoes stuffed with rice and flavoured with garlic, parsley and oregano. Found in the centre and south, they are baked with

Tomato sauce is a base used for many Italian dishes

sliced potatoes, which absorb the juices and make a tasty summer lunch.

Pomodori, al ✪

Tomato sauce flavoured either with onion or garlic and basil.

Porceddu ✪✪✪

Suckling pig roasted whole on the spit. Basted in its own juices to make the crackling crisp, the meat inside remains tender and succulent. When in the Sardianian countryside you must seek out this traditional dish in local restaurants.

Porchetta ✪✪✪

Roast pig, killed at about six or seven months and stuffed with garlic, rosemary, ground black pepper and grated pecorino cheese. It is sliced cold with a little stuffing and a piece of crunchy crackling. *Porchetta* is sold on roadside stalls that also supply the bread. Some also provide a few tables in the shade of the nearest tree, where you can enjoy your *porchetta* with a glass of local wine. Found in central Italy, especially near Rome.

Porcini ✪✪✪

Wild edible boletus mushrooms. They appear when the sun is still hot, after a cloudburst. August and September are the

Boletus mushurooms, gathered from the forests and woods of La Morra, Piedmont

ideal months, but unless you are an expert it can be very dangerous to pick your own. Fresh *porcini* are roasted or grilled whole with garlic and parsley. Dried, sliced *porcini* make delicious pasta sauces.

Prezzemolo

Parsley.

Profiteroles   ✪

A pile of small choux pastry puffs filled with whipped cream and coated with chocolate sauce. This sweet can be found in most good restaurants, especially in the north.

Prosciutto crudo   ✪✪✪

Italian cured ham. It is often referred to as Parma ham but there are, in fact, various types. The hams from Parma and Langhirano, for example, are medium-salty and very tasty, having been matured for a minimum of six months. San Daniele, from Friuli, is sweeter and has a more delicate flavour, while the *Prosciutto di montagna*, locally cured 'mountain' hams found in Tuscany, Umbria and Lazio, are decidedly saltier and have a stronger flavour; being still on the bone, they are carved by hand. Whichever you choose it must be freshly sliced, if it is not vacuum packed, as it changes its colour and flavour very quickly.

Prosciutto e melone or fichi   ✪✪✪

Paper-thin slices of PROSCIUTTO CRUDO served with wedges of chilled melon or peeled figs. The slightly salty flavour of the ham is balanced by the sweetness of the fruit. Although a summer starter, it is good served with a plate of pasta.

Provolone   ✪✪

A cows' milk cheese with a mild (*dolce*) or strong (*piccante*) flavour, depending on its maturity. The huge oblong cheeses are first cut into round slices, then into portions.

Puntarelle   ✪✪✪

Dark-green, leafy salad vegetable, with thick, fleshy stalks. You can find this vegetable in Rome in wintertime. The stalks are sliced thinly lengthways and dropped into iced water to make them curl. They are then dressed with oil, garlic, crushed anchovy fillets and vinegar. Basketfuls of ready prepared ones can be found at markets for a little extra charge.

Puttanesca, alla   ✪✪✪

Sauce made with tomatoes, black olives, capers, garlic and anchovy fillets. Often spiced with chillies, and traditionally served with spaghetti and chopped parsley.

Q

Quaglie 😊
Quails. These small game birds are usually grilled. They have a mild flavour, but watch out for the tiny bones.

Quattro formaggi, ai 😊😊
Sauce made from four different cheeses mixed with butter and cream.

R

Radicchio 😊😊😊
Red-leaved chicory. It has quite a bitter taste. Grown around Treviso in the north, it is served in salads or cut in half, grilled and dressed with olive oil and salt.

Ragú, al 😊😊
A rich Neopolitan meat sauce which has been cooked for at least four hours. Generally served with ZITI (traditional Neopolitan pasta), grated Parmesan and sometimes ricotta cheese.

Rane 😊
Frogs' legs. Popular in the north where they are often served as part of the FRITTO MISTO.

Ravanada 😊
A type of horseradish sauce served with BOLLITO MISTO in Trentino. It is freshly made from horseradish, sugar, vinegar and either grated apple or cream.

Ravioli 😊
Probably the best-known stuffed, square-shaped pasta. They can be stuffed with fish (*ravioli di magro* found in Liguria), with aubergines and nuts (*ravioli di melanzane* found in Sardinia) or with meat or ricotta cheese and spinach, like the ravioli found everywhere.

Ribollita 😊😊😊
Thick, Tuscan vegetable soup with beans and stale bread. The essential ingredient, however, is the locally grown black cabbage that gives the slightly sour taste.

Ribes
Redcurrants. Best in summer.

Ricciarelli 😊😊
Small marzipan cakes from Siena, sometimes covered in chocolate. Traditionally eaten at Christmas.

Ricotta 😊😊😊
Soft, white, unsalted cheese. *Ricotta romana* is a fresh cheese, originally made from ewes' milk, nowadays often mixed with cows' milk. The name *ricotta* means 'recooked', as it is made from the whey left over from cheese-making, which is reheated. On coagulation, the flakes of cheese are skimmed off, put into small

Pasta is stuffed and cut into square shapes to make famous ravioli

63

baskets and left to drain until the next day. Look out for the genuine ricotta sold by shepherds.

Rigatoni
A short, ribbed pasta.

Ris e verz ✪✪
Rice and cabbage soup from Lombardy. It is served with chopped parsley, ground black pepper and grated Parmesan.

Risi e bisi ✪✪✪
Rice and peas. A traditional Venetian dish served with grated Parmesan. Should be tried when in Venice.

Riso
Rice. One of the essential ingredients in Italian cuisine, it is served as RISOTTO, or rice salad, mixed with a sauce, added to soups or made into savoury balls and fried (SUPPLI). Grown in Piedmont, Lombardy, Emilia-Romagna and Veneto, it is classified into four categories: *originario*, the smallest grain, *semifino*, *fino* and *superfino*, the longest.

Risotto
A classic Italian savoury rice dish. Various ingredients are cooked together with the rice and stock is added gradually during the cooking until the rice is just cooked. It can be flavoured with vegetables such as mushrooms or artichokes, with fish or shellfish or with meat or sausage. (See box below.)

Robiola ✪
A mild, creamy cheese with a reddish rind, made in Lombardy and Piedmont. The best ones come from the pre-alpine valleys of Lombardy, where they are still matured in mountain caves.

Rognone trifolato ✪
Calf's kidney, sliced thinly and sautéed in olive oil, wine and onions.

Rosmarino
Rosemary. With its small, needle-like leaves and penetrating perfume, this herb is used to flavour roasts.

Rughetta ✪✪✪
A strong-flavoured, dark green leafy salad vegetable. Either picked wild or grown in allotments, it is excellent mixed with salads and tastes vaguely like watercress.

Rustico ✪
All savoury pastries and breads are known by this name. Filled with cheese, salami or ham, they are made in the home around Easter, especially in the south.

S

Salame ✪✪✪
Salami – a highly seasoned sausage made from pork, sometimes mixed with beef. The

Pea and asparagus, one of many risotto variations

MONARCH OF RICE DISHES

The exact ingredients of risotto may well vary according to the seasons or the mood of the chef but the result is moist and rather creamy. These are the most common combinations.

✪✪✪ **Risotto ai funghi** with mushrooms, often PORCINI (see recipe on page 108).

✪✪ **Risotto al Barolo** with the famous red Barolo wine.

✪✪ **Risotti alla crema di scampi** with cream and prawns or scampi.

✪✪ **Risotto alla Mantovana** or alla piolta with crumbled salami, butter and Parmesan.

✪✪✪ **Risotto alla Milanese** can be traced back to the 16th century when an unknown painter, working on the Duomo of Milan, fell in love with his master's daughter. At his wedding feast, he served this yellow risotto, coloured with the saffron used in his paints! Since then, this Milanese speciality has been cooked with bone marrow and meat stock and coloured and flavoured with saffron.

✪✪✪ **Risotto alla pescatora** with squid, prawns, mussels and clams. Often spiced with chilli.

✪✪ **Risotto alla Valdostana** with melted Fontina cheese and wine.

✪✪ **Risotto al nero di seppie** is flavoured and coloured black with ink sacks from cuttlefish. The fish are also chopped up in the rice.

Try the local salami, its delicious with freshly baked bread

meat is minced or chopped with pork fat and combined with wine, peppercorns, garlic and spices such as fennel seeds or chillies. This mixture is then forced into tubular bags, made from natural fibres, which are tied at each end and left to marinate in brine before being hung in a cool, dry place to mature. Some are smoked. Each region has its own type of salami. Ask the local butcher if he makes his own: these 'home-made' ones are really tasty.

Sale

Salt.

Salmone

Salmon.

Salsa

Sauce. Usually refers to the uncooked variety such as mayonnaise.

Salsicce ✪✪

Sausage. Italian sausages are very spicy. Nearly every region has its own speciality, but the best ones, like the salami, are made by the village butcher. Best grilled over a wood or charcoal fire, they are

66

often served with beans or a green vegetable that has been sautéed in oil, with garlic and chilli pepper. They are also served in a tomato sauce with pasta or POLENTA. It is difficult to find a *trattoria* without sausages on the menu.

Saltimbocca alla romana ✪✪✪

A very tasty Roman dish made from thin veal escalopes flavoured with cured ham and sage, and cooked in butter and wine. It is so good that it 'jumps in your mouth' – the meaning of *saltimbocca* (see recipe on page 109).

Salvia

Sage. Fresh and dried sage can be found at the greengrocer's. The greyish green, velvety leaves of this herb have a strong flavour and should be used sparingly.

Sanguinaccio ✪✪

A dense chocolate spread found in the south when pigs are slaughtered. Made from pigs' blood that has been cooked with sugar, chocolate and pieces of candied peel and flavoured with cinammon and vanilla. It is eaten with sponge fingers as a sweet. The home-made version is best, but you can also find it at the grocer's.

Saor ✪✪
A Venetian sauce made from onion, vinegar, spices, pine kernels and sultanas. It is used for marinating fish.

Sarago
White bream.

Sarde
Sardines.

Sarde a 'beccaficu' ✪✪✪
Sardines, 'fig-pecker' style. They are boned, stuffed, dipped in flour and beaten egg, then fried with their tails left on so that they resemble the small birds they are named after. The filling varies from town to town: breadcrumbs, cheese and tomatoes in some places, onion, sultanas and pine kernels in others. A symbol of Sicily, they must be tried on a visit to the island.

Sartú di riso ✪✪✪
A rice pie from Naples. A 'crust' of rice cooked with a rich RAGÙ sauce is filled with layers of mozzarella, hard-boiled eggs, chicken livers, sliced sausage, peas, mushrooms and more *ragú* sauce. This rich, elaborate dish is becoming increasingly difficult to find.

Sardines are caught of the coast around Sicily

Sauté di vongole ✪✪✪
Fresh clams (VONGOLE) cooked in oil and garlic until their shells open, served with lashings of chopped parsley. Delicious served with fresh, crusty bread as a starter or summer main course.

Sbrisolona, la ✪✪
A traditional cake from Mantua, which looks and tastes rather like a 'crumble', with the addition of finely chopped almonds.

Scaloppine ✪✪
Escalopes, usually veal. The thin slices of veal are typically, dipped in seasoned flour and fried in butter or olive oil. *Scaloppine* can be flavoured with lemon juice (*al limone*), white wine (*al vino*), or a sweet, sherry-like wine (*al Marsala*). Easy to prepare, they can be found in most restaurants.

Scamorza ✪✪✪
A cows' milk cheese which is similar to mozzarella but is slightly matured. It is often served grilled, when it becomes crusty on the outside and soft in the centre.

Sciatt ✪✪
Little fritters flavoured with BITTO cheese and GRAPPA liqueur and fried in butter or lard. They are served piping hot as a starter. A delicious treat from Valtellina in Lombardy.

Seadas ✪✪✪
A light pastry case filled with a mild cheese and served warm, coated with honey. This typical Sardinian dessert is a rather unusual taste experience!

Sedano
Celery.

Seppie coi piselli ✪✪
Also known as *seppie alla romana*. A traditional Roman dish of cuttlefish cooked in tomato sauce and served with freshly boiled peas.

Sfogliatelle di Santa Rosa ✪✪✪
Crispy cakes filled with custard cream. Every year, at the end of July or beginning of August, in Conca dei Marini near Salerno, there is a *festa* in honour of these cakes. Originally made by the cloistered nuns of St Rose's convent who offered them to the poor on St Rose's Day.

Sfogliatelle napoletane ✪✪✪
Small cakes made either from a type of crisp puff pastry and called *ricce* or from short-crust and called *frolle*. Both are filled with sweetened ricotta cheese and candied peel,

67

and flavoured with vanilla and cinammon. If you are ever in Naples early in the morning, your nose will lead you to the nearest cake shop taking the first batch of *sfogliatelle* out of the oven. An irresistable mid-morning snack.

Sgavecio ⭐⭐

A Ligurian dish of small fish which have been fried and pickled in vinegar and wine with onions and spices.

Soffritto ⭐⭐

A Neapolitan speciality made from pigs' offal cooked in tomato purée, oil, lard and chilli pepper and flavoured with bay leaves and rosemary. It is served with spaghetti or toast.

Sogliola

Sole.

Sopa cauda ⭐⭐

Soup made from layers of bread and boned pigeon, covered with broth. Traditionally served in the Veneto in an earthenware pot, it is more like a 'pudding' than a soup!

Soppressata ⭐⭐

Salami made from pig's head and tongue with spices and pistachio nuts. It can be found in most grocers' and butchers' shops in Tuscany. *Soppressata* means 'pressed'. Many more varieties can be found, especially in the south, all called by the same name.

Sorrentina, alla ⭐⭐

Sauce made with tomatoes and basil, from Sorrento. Cubes of mozzarella cheese are added when mixing the sauce with the pasta. Served with grated Parmesan.

Spaghetti

Long, thin pasta, the word means 'little strings'. Some find this pasta rather difficult to eat. The secret is not to wind too much around your fork at once, and then pop it into your mouth before it has a chance to unwind. Italian etiquette is still undecided whether you can use a spoon.

Speck ⭐⭐⭐

A smoked cured ham from Alto Adige. It is served as a starter with other cooked meats. Delicious vacuum-packed, home-cured hams can be bought all over the region – a treat for smoked meat fans.

Spezzatino ⭐

A stew, usually made with young beef or veal cooked in a tomato sauce. It is served with potatoes and peas. There is also a version without tomatoes, cooked in white wine.

Spiedini ⭐

Skewers filled with various combinations of meat, fish and vegetables.

Spigola

Bass.

Spuntino

Snack.

Stelline

Small pasta stars served in BRODO and a favourite with children.

Stinco di maiale al forno ⭐⭐⭐

A whole pork shank, from knee to trotter (not with trotter), per person, roasted in the oven with garlic, rosemary and wine. It is cooked until the meat becomes tender and succulent, while the crackling becomes crisp and crunchy. It is better not to order anything for starters as it is too good to leave on your plate. A speciality from Trentino-Alto Adige.

Stoccafisso ⭐⭐⭐

This dried cod is often confused with the salted cod called BACCALÀ. It is imported from Norway. The stiff fish can be seen hanging in grocers' shops or on market stalls. It has to be soaked for several days before it can be cooked. *Stoccafisso* has a very strong flavour – stronger than BACCALÀ – and it is not to everyone's taste. See also BACALA ALLA VICENTINA and BACALÀ MANTECATO.

Stracchino ⭐

A fresh, creamy, fat cheese made from cows' milk, with a very mild flavour which soon turns bitter when kept too long. Sold in individual wrapped portions, it is ideal for spreading on rolls.

Spaghetti bolognese, a trademark of Italian cuisine

Stracciatella ❶
A thin Roman soup made by stirring a mixture of beaten egg and grated cheese into boiling BRODO. It is then served with more grated cheese if liked.

Stracotto ❷
A joint of lean beef, larded with streaky bacon, and braised with onion, a little tomato purée and wine in an earthenware pot for four hours. Literally translated, *stracotto* means 'overcooked', and the meat is so tender that it melts in your mouth. Served with potato purée or POLENTA, it is a traditional dish from Lombardy and Emilia-Romagna.

Strangolapreti ❷
Tiny dumplings made from breadcrumbs, spinach, sultanas and pine kernels. In Trentino, they are served with melted butter and grated cheese. In the south, the curious name of 'priest chokers' refers to GNOCCHI made from flour and water and served with RAGÙ sauce.

Strudel ❶
Apple, nut and sultana strudel pastry roll, spiced with cinammon. Can be found all over Trentino-Alto Adige where it is sold whole, or in portions topped with whipped cream.

Tagliatelle-maker at work – it's not as easy as it looks

Struffoli ❷
A Neapolitan Christmas sweet made from tiny balls of fried pastry covered with honey and decorated with candied peel, glacé cherries and 'hundreds and thousands'.

Sugo
Pasta sauce. There are hundreds of different pasta sauces; new ones are invented every day, *Aglio, olio peperoncino* is one of the simplest, containing oil, garlic and chillies (see recipe on page 103). The most common appear alphabetically within the A–Z listing.

Suppli ❸
Deep-fried savoury rice balls. Made from rice cooked in tomato and meat sauce, rolled into egg-shaped balls with mozzarella cheese, dipped in egg and breadcrumbs, then deep fried. A Roman speciality, they make a wonderful filler while waiting for your pizza.

T

Tacchino
Turkey.

Tagliatelle
Familiar egg noodles. May be green (verde) and flavoured with spinach.

Taleggio ❷
Tasty, ivory-coloured cheese, made in large, flat squares. It was originally made in Val Taleggio but can now be found all over the north. Its flavour resembles Camembert and gets stronger as it matures.

Taralli ❸
Savoury ring-shaped biscuits from Naples. They are made with pork dripping and lots of ground black pepper. Strands of dough are twisted together, with whole blanched almonds pushed in at random to roast while the biscuits bake. They are delicious as a snack with a glass of chilled wine.

Tartine ❶
Canapés with truffle, chicken liver or olive pâté. Served hot or cold as a starter.

Tartufo ❸
White and black truffles. A real delicacy, they grow underground. Armed with a torch and trowel, the truffle 'hunter' goes out at night to avoid being seen digging in his 'secret' place, where specially trained dogs have sniffed out a find. The more prestigious white truffle (*tartufo bianco*) from Alba in Piedmont, can grow as big as an orange, and

Truffles, the world's most expensive foodstuff

is found in Umbria. Both have a strong flavour and intense, penetrating perfume, should be used sparingly, and are grated on to risottos, salads and sauces.

Tiella
The local dialect for 'baking tin' in Apulia, where many dishes are layered with potatoes and baked in the oven.

Tiella di sardine ✪✪
Tiella made with sardines (*sarde*). Beaten egg and grated cheese are poured over before the dish is baked until golden.

Tiramisù ✪✪✪
A deliciously rich dessert made from sponge fingers soaked in strong black coffee, then layered with brandy-flavoured whipped cream and eggs (see recipe on page 116).

Tomini ✪✪
Small individual fresh cheeses made in Piedmont. They have a very delicate flavour and are served with oilve oil and ground black pepper as a starter or to end a meal. The adventurous may like to try *tomini elettrici* marinated in oil, vinegar, chopped garlic and chillies.

Tonno
Tuna.

Tonno, al ✪✪
Sauce made with tomatoes and tuna, often spiced with chillies. Traditionally served with spaghetti and chopped parsley.

Tonno e fagioli ✪✪
Canned tuna mixed with cannellini beans, onion and parsley and dressed with olive oil and vinegar or lemon juice. A delicious snack (see recipe on page 113).

Tonno e pomodoro ✪
A salad made from sliced tomatoes, hard-boiled eggs, new potatoes and tuna dressed with ground black pepper and oilve oil. A quickly prepared tasty summer snack.

Torta di mandorle ✪
Sponge cake filled with apricot jam, moistened with liqueur and covered with piped almond paste. It is one of the most common cakes.

Torta Pasqualina ✪✪✪
Puff pastry case filled with either beet tops or artichokes mixed with beaten eggs and cheese. From Liguria, it is served traditionally at Easter.

Tortelli di zucca ✪✪✪
An unusual stuffed pasta, filled with sweetened pumpkin, from Mantua. Served with melted butter and grated Parmesan, it is definately for sweet-and-sour lovers.

Tortellini ✪✪✪
Ring-shaped pasta stuffed with a meat mixture. A speciality of Emilia-Romagna, it is served either in BRODO, with melted butter

71

and cheese or with meat sauce. Delicious with cream.

Tortiglioni

This is a pasta similar to RIGATONI, but curved and twisted instead of ribbed.

Totani ripieni ✪✪

A member of the squid family with a slightly sweeter flavour than squid. In Sicily they are stuffed with a savoury breadcrumb mixture and baked on a bed of sliced lemons. In Apulia, they are baked with potatoes, while in Tuscany you will find them stuffed with greens and casseroled with chillies.

Tozzetti ✪✪

Small, hard biscuits made with hazelnuts and almonds. Served in Tuscany with a glass of Vin Santo (sweet wine).

Trenette

A type of 'flattened' spaghetti. It is traditionally served with PESTO. Also called *linguine*.

Triglie

Red mullet.

Triglie alla livornese ✪✪✪

Red mullet, Leghorn style. The fish are fried in oil and chillies and served in a tomato sauce with chopped parsley.

Trippa

Tripe.

Trippa alla romana ✪✪✪

Tripe cooked in a dense tomato and vegetable sauce flavoured with mint and served with lashings of grated pecorino cheese. It can be found in the *osterie* in Rome on Saturdays – tripe day there.

Trota

Trout.

Trota spaccata ✪✪

'Split' trout, from Valle d'Aosta. The fish are split in two, dipped in flour and fried in spiced butter. This butter is then used to dress the trout when served with chopped parsley.

U

Uccelli scappati ✪✪

Kebabs, called 'flown birds', made with pieces pork, pork liver and sausage, divided by sage leaves. They are browned in butter, sprinkled with wine, cooked until tender and served with POLENTA.

Uova

Eggs.

Uva

Grapes. Best in summer.

Tiramisu, *a tempting desert for those with a sweet tooth*

V

Freshly harvested white turnips

Verdura
Vegetables.

Vermicelli
Thin pasta worms. These are often called SPAGHETTI even though they are, in fact, slightly fatter. In Naples they are traditionally served with fish sauces.

Vincisgrassi ✪✪✪
A pasta dish. One of the oldest dishes from The Marches. It is similar to lasagne except that the meat sauce is made from chicken giblets, minced beef and pork. It is heavily flavoured with marjoram.

Vincotto ✪
A delicious spread made by slowly boiling down grape juice until it reaches the consistancy of honey. Used for making cakes or spreading on bread, like jam.

Vitello tonnato ✪
Thinly sliced veal coated with tuna mayonnaise flavoured with anchovies and capers. This cold, summer dish, originating from the north, is a fresh-tasting main course for a hot summer evening.

Vongole
Clams. The most common shellfish, sold by the kilo at the fishmonger's. Buy those in the date-stamped net bags: they have been oficially checked for disease.

Vongole, alle ✪✪✪
Sauce made with clams, with or without tomatoes. Traditionally served with spaghetti and chopped parsley.

W

Wurstel ✪
Frankfurter sausages. Made from a mixture of pork and beef, they are very popular served with sauerkraut in the *birrerie* (beer houses), sliced for sandwich fillings and chopped up in rice salads.

Z

Zabaione or zabaglione ✪✪✪
A kind of cooked syllabub made from whisking fresh egg yolks with sugar and Marsala (a sweet wine similar to sherry). It is served with sponge fingers as a sweet or 'pick-me-up' (see recipe on page 116).

Zafferano
Saffron. Can be bought in tiny packets from the grocer's. A little

73

goes a long way. An essential ingredient in RISOTTO ALLA MILANESE.

Zampone ✪✪✪

A highly spiced sausage in a bag shaped like a pig's trotter (*zampone*). It is boiled and served sliced, with lentils, at New Year.

Zeppole ✪✪

A type of fried doughnut rolled in cinnamon and sugar, found in the *friggitorie* (fried food shops) in Naples and the south. Traditionally they are made to celebrate St Joseph's day, when they are topped with custard cream and a sour cherry.

Ziti

A long, tubular pasta. It has to be broken up into shorter lengths before cooking. Traditionally served with Neapolitan RAGÙ.

Zucchini

Courgettes.

Zuppa

Soup. Some of the most popular are listed below.

Zuppa di cozze ✪✪✪

Mussel soup. It is made by cooking mussels in their own juice, then adding tomatoes, oil, garlic and parsley. Served with crusty bread.

Zuppa di fagioli ✪✪

A thick soup made from beans, cooked and flavoured according to regional recipes.

Zuppa di lenticchie ✪✪

Thick lentil soup, usually flavoured with ham and served with croûtons.

Zuppa di pesce ✪✪✪

Spicy fish soup found on the coast in the south. It is made from a mixture of seafood, shellfish and fish, the essential ingredient being scorpion fish (*scorfano*), which gives the characteristic flavour. The fish are all cooked with tomatoes, oil, wine, garlic and chilli, then served with croûtons. A deliciously filling one-course meal, but watch out for the bones!

Zuppa d'orzo ✪✪

A thick barley and potato soup flavoured with pork and bacon. A warming dish from the Valle d'Aosta.

Zuppa inglese ✪

'English soup'. It is in fact a dessert and can be compared to trifle. Sponge cake is soaked in liqueur, layered with custard cream and covered with whipped cream. Found in most restaurants especially central regions.

Zuppa pavese ✪✪✪

A couple of eggs poached in boiling BRODO, which is poured over slices of fried bread. It is served in individual dishes with lashings of grated Parmesan cheese. This typical soup from Lombardy was first offered to King Francis I of France after his defeat at the Battle of Pavia in 1525. A farmer's wife, having only bread and broth to offer the monarch, had the brilliant idea of adding two freshly laid eggs to make a dish fit for a king!

Mussel soup is an excellent light lunch

Wine &
Drink of
Italy

Above: *Il Corno wine
    cellar in Tuscany*
Right: *a satisfied grape
    picker*

Wine & Drink of Italy

Italian wines are not as well known interna-
tionally as they should be. Until about 20 years
ago they were poorly promoted, leaving France
to dominate the market. However, in the last decade they have
regained lost ground and many of the best wines now prevail
over their French counterparts.

To protect the image of their wines, the Italians followed the
excellent example of the French *Appellation d'Origine
Contrôlée* and, in 1963, introduced the DOC system –
Denominazione di Origine Controllata. This guarantees the
origin of each wine that, once approved, may display DOC on
its label. A further guarantee was introduced in 1980 – the
DOCG, *Denominazione di Origine Controllata e Garantita* only
given to outstanding wines. There are, however, some
excellent table wines that come into neither category, and the
local *vino sfuso*, loose wine sold by the litre, or the *vino della
casa* served in jugs in *trattorie*, is often pleasant.

Italy, thanks to its many spas, produces over 200 brands of
mineral water. Most are claimed to have diuretic properties,
thus aiding digestion. And be sure to try Italian firewaters like
grappa, as well as aperitifs such as Cinzano and Campari.
Dinner must be followed by a cup of the Italian national drink:
richly roasted black coffee and perhaps a thimble of what
Italians call a *digestivo* (a liqueur).

Harvesting the famous Chanti grapes

Wine Producing Regions

DOG is a method of classification that guarantees the origin of the wine, and that it has been made following the guidelines for a particular area. However, it is no indication of quality. Sample the local wines or house wines as well, and treat yourself to more famous tipples in the appropriate regions.

The main wines found in each region are listed below and the more interesting ones are described in more detail.

PIEDMONT AND VALLE D'AOSTA

Dry red: Barbaresco, Barbera, Barolo, Dolcetto, Gattinara, Grignolino, Nebbiolo.
Dry white: Cortese, Erbaluce, Gavi.
Sparkling: Asti Spumante.

Asti Spumante DOC

A sparkling wine which is pale to golden yellow, sweet with typical aromatic flavour of Moscato grapes. Best served 'on ice'. Although some historians attribute the origin of this world-famous wine to Pope Leo X de' Medici (1475–1521), a great *spumante* lover, it was Carlo Gancia in 1850 who officially created it by adopting the French *méthode champenoise* to compete with Champagne.

Barbaresco DOCG

Garnet red with orange reflections, this 'stern', full-bodied wine is dry and smooth. It is best served at room temperature with roasts and other red meat or game. This so-called twin of Barolo, comes from the borough of Barbaresco, south of Asti. A legend recounts that the inhabitants of the area, during the invasion of the Moors, plied their oppressors with the local red wine. The barbarians' got so drunk that the local people were able to cut their throats while they were asleep. The wine has been called Barbaresco ever since. It must age for at least two years; after three it can be called *Riserva*, after four *Riserva Speciale*, but it should not be kept for more than ten years.

Barolo DOCG

Garnet red with orange reflections, this, like Barbaresco, is a stern, full-bodied wine which is dry and smooth. Best served at room temperature, uncorked at least three hours previously, with roasted red meats, game and rich truffled sauces. This wine, produced in the area around Barolo, a small village half-way between Turin and Cuneo, was first made in the 19th century in the vineyard of the Marquis of Barolo, still one of the largest producers. Barolo improves with age and is ready for drinking at three years old; after five, it can be called *Riserva*.

Gavi DOC

Pale yellow with a hint of green, this wine is fresh and dry, Best served chilled with starters, salads, fish and poultry and is also excellent as an aperitif. Also known as *Cortese di Gavi*, it is made from the Cortese grapes which grow to the south of Alessandria. Being one of the best Italian white wines, it is often served at official banquets and on special occasions. Gavi should be drunk before it is two years old; it is also available as a dry *spumante*.

LOMBARDY

Dry red: Oltrepò Pavese, Riviera del Garda Bresciano, San Colombano, Valtellina.
Dry white: Franciacorta, Tocai San Martino della Battaglia, Valcalepio.

Franciacorta DOC

Pale yellow with greenish reflections, this wine tastes dry and agreeably savoury. Best served chilled with fish dishes. Makes an excellent aperitif. The name goes back to medieval times when the land where it was produced was freed from vassallage and called Franca Curtis. It is made mainly in Borgonato di Cortefranca, a medieval hamlet in the province of Brescia.

Oltrepò Pavese DOC

Ruby red in colour, this is a full-bodied, dry wine. Best served at about l8°C/65°F with boiled meats, stews, hams and salami,

Takes its name from the land 'across the river Po from Pavia', where it is produced. Best drunk when young.

Valtellina DOC

A ruby red wine which is dry and smooth. Best served at about 18°C/65°F with white meats and poultry. Produced in the Valtellina Valley around Sondrio. Best aged for at least a year. Valtellina *Superiore*, made in specific areas along the valley, should age for two years.

TRENTINO-ALTO ADIGE

Dry red: Cabernet, Caldaro, Marzemino, Merlot, Pinot Nero.

Dry white: Pinot Bianco, Riesling, Terlano, Traminer Aromatico del Trentino.

Marzemino DOC

Dark ruby red with orange reflections, it is a full-bodied, dry and bitterish wine. Best served at room temperature with POLENTA, RAVIOLI, red and white meats and poultry. This jewel of Trentino wines is not very well known. Mozart, however, was so impressed that he mentioned it in his opera *Don Giovanni*.

Riesling DOC

Very pale yellow wine with a greenish tinge. It tastes dry, fruity and agreeably acidulous (or slightly tangy). Best served slightly chilled with fish, crustaceans and starters. The three similar Riesling wines made from three Riesling vines, *Italico*, *Renano* and *Sylvaner*, are all bottled in the traditional long, slim bottle.

Traminer Aromatico del Trentino DOC

Pale yellow verging on golden, this wine is dry, intense and typically aromatic. Best served slightly chilled with fish soups and seafood. It has such a characteristic taste and bouquet that, once tasted, it will never be forgotten.

VENETO

Dry red: Bardolino, Cabernet, Colli Euganei, Merlot, Valpolicella.

Dry white: Gambellara, Soave.

Medium-sweet red: Recioto della Valpolicella.

Sweet: Vin Santo di Gambellara.

Recioto della Valpolicella DOC

A garnet red wine with a medium-sweet (*amabile*), warm and smooth taste. Best served with dessert. Made from the same vines as Valpolicella but using the ripest and sweetest grapes. Once harvested, they are left to dry and sweeten further in the sun before pressing.

Soave DOC

Pale yellow with a greenish hint, this is a dry harmonious wine with a slight almondy aftertaste. Best served chilled with seafood or egg dishes. Soave is produced in the province of Verona, and legend has it that Romeo and Juliet were sampling a goblet of local wine together when he muttered *'Soave!'*, which Juliet took to be an endearment, *'My sweet'!*, whereas he was simply showing his appreciation of the sweet, soft wine!

Valpolicella DOC

Ruby red turning to garnet on ageing, this is a full-bodied, dry wine. Best served at room temperature with all meats, game and cheeses. Ernest Hemingway was so taken by the quality of this everyday wine that he mentioned it frequently in his book *Across the River and Into the Trees*. It should be drunk within five years.

FRIULI-VENEZIA GIULIA

Dry red: Grave del Friuli, Merlot, Refosco.

Dry white: Collio Goriziano, Pinot Grigio, Tocai, Sauvignon.

Medium-sweet white: Picolit.

Picolit DOC

A pale yellow wine with a medium-sweet or sweet taste, agreeable and delicate. Best served chilled with desserts and strong-flavoured cheeses. This is one of the rarest and most expensive wines on the market, as it is produced in limited quantities, the vine not being very prolific. It is always present at state banquets.

Pinot Grigio DOC
Golden yellow with coppery reflections, this is a dry, full-bodied wine with a slight after-taste of bitter almonds. Best served slightly chilled with starters, fish, pasta, risottos and white meats, Pinot Grigio can be found in various parts of the north where it varies slightly from region to region, depending on climatic and geographical conditions.

Tocai DOC
A bright, pale yellow wine with golden reflections. It tastes dry and aromatic. Best served slightly chilled with starters, and egg and fish dishes. Mixed with bitter Campari, soda water and lemon peel, and served with an olive, it makes an excellent local aperitif called *Spitz*.

LIGURIA
Cinque Terre DOC
Pale yellow in colour, this is a dry wine, typically aromatic. Best served at about 10°C/50°F with fish dishes such as BURIDDA. The five villages of the Cinque Terre cling like limpets to the rocky cliffs north of La Spezia. The vines are miraculously cultivated on terraces cut into the rock, starting at sea-level and climbing up to 800m/2,600ft. Best drunk within the year, and within a maximum of two years.

EMILIA-ROMAGNA
Dry red: Colli Bolognesi, Gutturnio Colli Piacentini, Sangiovese di Romagna.
Dry white: Bianco di Scandiano, Trebbiano di Romagna.
Sparkling: Lambrusco di Sorbara.

Lambrusco di Sorbara DOC
Ruby red, this wine is dry or medium-sweet (*amabile*) and sparkling. Not to be confused with white and rosé alternatives available back home: this red wine is full of Italian character. Best served at I5°C/60°F when

dry, with salami, cured hams, stuffed pastas; cooler when sweet, with desserts. Lambrusco DOC is naturally sparkling; the table wine often has added gas.

Sangiovese di Romagna DOC
A ruby red wine with a smooth and dry taste, and an agreeably bitterish aftertaste. Best served at 18°C/65°F with poultry, white meats and egg dishes.

Christened *Sanguis Jovis* (Blood of Jupiter) by a monk, when asked by a monastery guest for the name of the local wine he found so agreeable, this wine has since been known as *Sangiovese*. Best enjoyed while relatively young, but not before April of the year following its production.

TUSCANY
Dry red: Brunello di Montalcino, Chianti, Morellino di Scansano, Parrina, Vino Nobile di Montepulciano.
Dry white: Bianco di Pitigliano, Bianco Valdinievole, Elba, Galestro, Parrina, Vernaccia di San Gimignano.
Rosato: Rosatello Ruffino.
Sweet: Vin Santo.

Brunello di Montalcino DOCG
Deep ruby red tending to garnet on ageing, this is a smooth, dry and warm wine. Best served between 20° and 22°C/68°–71°F, with roasts, game and liver. The bottle should be uncorked several hours previously and the wine decanted.

This aristocratic wine, revered by connois-seurs, was the first to be granted DOCG status. The time, patience and fond loving care needed in production explains not only the very high quality but also the high price of this wine. It can age for up to 50 years in the right conditions.

Chianti DOCG
Bright ruby red, this is a wine which is dry, sapid (pleasantly characterful), slightly tannic, becoming smoother with age. This is a wine best served at room temperature with

roasts, grilled meats, game and salami.

In 1924, the small vineyards making the *Chianti Classico*, in the original Chianti-producing area from south of Florence (Firenze) to north of Siena, formed a *consorzio* (association), with a black cock as their symbol, to protect themselves against imitation.

There are another two *consorzi* defending the good name of Chianti made in other areas: Centauro and Putto. Bettino Ricasoli, known as the Iron Baron and one of the fathers of Italian Renaissance, established the proportions of the different grapes used to make the modern Chianti. It is still produced on a large scale by the Ricasoli family at their castle in Brolio. Chianti is best drunk within four years, unless it is *Riserva* when it will last for six.

Galestro

Very pale greenish yellow wine with a clean, dry and fresh taste. Best served chilled with summer dishes and fish. It also makes an excellent aperitif.

A relatively new table wine which takes its name from the grey *galestro* rock (marl) which is found in the area. Its low alcohol content and 'cheerful' character have met with success.

Vernaccia di San Gimignano DOC

Pale golden yellow, this wine is smooth, dry and slightly bitterish. Best served chilled with starters, fish and seafood. It was the first to be granted the status of DOC and one of the most mentioned wines in history. Pope Paul III Farnese bathed in it; Michelangelo sang its praises; Boccaccio dreamed about streams of it; Saint Catherine of Siene and her fellow sisters used it as medicine; and Dante sent Pope Martin IV to purgatory because of it in his *Divina Commedia*.

UMBRIA

Dry red: Colli del Trasimeno, Colli Perugini.
Dry white: Colli del Trasimeno, Orvieto DOC.

Orvieto DOC

A pale golden yellow wine with a dry or medium-sweet (*abboccato*) taste. Best served chilled, with fish when dry, or with freshwater fish and egg dishes when *abboccato*. The medium-sweet wine has a typical bitter-almond flavour and saffron bouquet. The dry wine is produced to satisfy market demand. Both wines are best drunk within two years of production.

THE MARCHE

Dry red: Rosso del Conero, Rosso Piceno.
Dry white: Bianchello del Metauro, Falerio dei Colli Ascolani, Verdicchio dei Castelli di Jesi.

Rosso del Conero DOG

A ruby red, full-bodied and dry wine. Best served at 18°C/65°F, the bottle having been uncorked two hours before serving, with poultry and casseroled meats. Takes its name from Mount Conero, the picturesque rocky headland to the south of Ancona. It is a shame that this enjoyable wine is not better known outside its area of production.

Verdicchio dei Castelli di Jesi DOC

Soft, pale yellow in colour, this dry and harmonious wine has an agreeably bitterish aftertaste. Best served chilled with starters and local fish dishes.

One of the best white wines which takes its name from the greenish-yellow colour of the grapes from which it is made, this is best enjoyed young, while its cousin, the *Verdicchio* from Matelica, will withstand a life of two years.

LAZIO

Dry red: Colle Picchioni 'Vigna del Vassallo', Olevano, Velletri.
Dry white: Est! Estl! Est!!! di Montefiascone, Frascati, Colli Albani, Marino, Velletri.
Sweet: Aleatico di Gradoli, Olevano Rosso.
Spuzuante: Olevano.

Colle Picchioni 'Vigna del Vassallo'

Bright ruby red with garnet reflections, this wine is dry and smooth with a 'lively character'. Best served at room temperature with roasts of red or white meat. A relatively new wine produced by a family-run business. It has already received great acclaim from wine connoisseurs at home and abroad, and is considered one of the best red wines in Italy today. Best enjoyed before it reaches the age of eight or ten years, depending on the vintage. The dry white Colle Picchioni *Le Vignole* is worth seeking out, too.

Est! Est!! Est!!! di Montefiascone DOC

A bright, pale yellow wine which is full-bodied and dry or medium-sweet (*abboccato*).

Best served at around 10°C/50°F with pasta, fried dishes and fish.

Produced on the shores of Lake Bolsena, this wine owes its name to Martin, a young page, who was sent ahead of his master to seek out inns serving good wine. He was so enthusiastic about the one in Montefiascone that he wrote the agreed signal three times (*'Est!'* indicated the presence of good wine).

Frascati DOC

A brilliant pale yellow wine with a dry and slightly aromatic taste. Best served between 9° and 12°C/48°–54°F with starters, fish, salami, cheeses, vegetables and Roman cuisine. Considered the 'wine of Rome', it is served in typical litre measures in the *osterie*. Best enjoyed locally when young,

ABRUZZO AND MOLISE

Dry red: Montepulciano d'Abruzzo.
Dry white: Trebbiano d'Abruzzo.

CAMPANIA

Dry red: Capri, Gragnano, Ischia, Per'è Palummo, Taurasi.
Dry white: Capri, Fiano di Avellino, Greco di Tufo, Ischia.

Greco di Tufo DOG

A pale yellow or golden wine with dry and harmonious taste. Best served between 8° and 10°C/46°–50°F with shellfish, crustaceans and fried fish.

A fresco in Pompei, has a poem by a rejected lover complaining about his partner's frigidity despite the Greco wine with which she had been plied the night before. Best drunk within five years.

APULIA

Dry red: Brindisi, Cacc'è Mmitte, Copertino, Primitivo di Manduria.
Dry white: Locorotondo, Martina Franca, San Severo.
Rosato: Brindisi, San Severo.
Sweet: Aleatico di Puglia, Primitivo di Manduria.

Cacc'è Mmitte DOC

Ruby red, this wine is dry and harmonious. Best served at 18°–20°C/65°–68°F with soups, white meats and salami. The unusual name, literally translated from the local dialect, means 'Get it out and put it in', referring to the inn-keeper who should keep drawing off wine from the barrel and filling up your glass. Best enjoyed within three or four years.

BASILICATA
Aglianico del Vulture DOC

Ruby red becoming brick red with age, this wine is dry, harmonious and extremely agreeable. Best served at room temperature, uncorked an hour before, with red meats, roasts, game and lamb. Takes its name from the Aglianico vines that grow on the slopes of the volcano Vulture. The wine, with its typical bouquet reminiscent of strawberries and raspberries, can be kept for up to 20 years. It is the only wine produced in Basilicata, but some say that it can be counted among the first ten red wines in Europe.

CALABRIA
Dry red: Cirò, Pollino, Savuto.
Dry white: Greco di Bianco, Melissa.

Cirò DOC
Ruby red tending to orange in colour, this is a warm, harmonious and dry wine. Best served at room temperature with roasted red meats, game and poultry.

Produced around Cirò and Cirò Marina on the Ionian coast, it was offered to winners of the Olympic Games from Magna Graecia (the ancient Greek colonies in southern Italy). More recently, it was offered to the Italian athletes competing in the 1968 Olympics in Mexico City. It should age for at least four years and some vintages can exceed ten.

SICILY
Dry red: Cerasuolo di Vittoria, Corvo.
Dry white: Alcamo, Corvo, Etna, Rapitalà.
Sweet: Malvasia delle Lipari, Marsala, Moscato di Pantelleria.

Marsala DOC
Dark amber in colour, this is generally a slightly syrupy wine. Best served as an aperitif.

Marsala was originally a normal wine, first shipped to England in 1773. To prevent it turning to vinegar during the long voyage, neat alcohol and concentrated must were added, The British, in fact, had a monopoly in production of Marsala until Vincenzo Florio decided that enough was enough and opened the first Sicilian winery alongside the British. Now produced in the west of Sicily, there are several types: dry, medium dry, sweet and *all'uovo* (with added egg yolks), often prescribed as a pick-me-up.

Moscato di Pantelleria DOC
From golden to amber in colour. this is a sweet, typically aromatic wine. Best served between 6° and 10°C/42°–50°F with desserts and cakes.

It is produced on the beautiful, remote, volcanic island of Pantelleria in the middle of the Mediterranean, where it is the main source of income, The wine is made from the very sweet Zibibbo grapes, with their characteristic cinnamon flavour. The grapes are left to dry in the sun until they reach a pre-raisin state and then pressed to make the famous Moscato Passito di Pantelleria, sweeter and even more alcoholic, sometimes reaching more than 23 per cent.

SARDINIA
Dry red: Cannonau, Carignano del Sulcis, Girò di Cagliari.
Dry white: Nasco di Cagliari, Nuragus, Vermentino di Gallura, Vernaccia di Oristano.
Sweet: Nasco di Cagliari, Girò di Cagliari.

Cannonau DOC
Ruby red, turning orangy on ageing, this is a dry to medium-sweet wine with a characteristic flavour, Best served at room temperature with red meats and game. Produced all over Sardinia and reflecting the different geographical and climatic characteristics of the island, its flavour changes slightly from place to place. A wine that is best enjoyed within four or five years.

Vermentino di Gallura DOC
Bright pale yellow with greenish reflections, this is a dry, slightly bitterish wine. Best served chilled as an aperitif or with starters and fish. This excellent, slightly sparkling wine is considered worthy of drinking with oysters! Should be consumed within two years of production.

Vernaccia di Oristano DOC
An amber-yellow wine with a dry, harmonious taste and a slight aftertaste of bitter almonds. Best served chilled as an aperitif or with crustaceans, especially crayfish and lobster. Vernaccia is virtually undrinkable until it has aged for at least two years in oak barrels. After ageing for another two years, it is transformed into a dessert wine, similar to sherry. One of the most famous of these is called Sardinian Gold, produced by the wine co-operative in Oristano.

A–Z of Italian Wine & Drink

A

Acqua
Water. This is perhaps one of the most useful words to know when sightseeing, as it can be a thirsty business in the heat! You will be given a glass in the bars with your coffee or ice-cream, and you can find plenty of drinking fountains in most cities and towns.

Acqua non potabile
This is water which is not suitable for drinking. If you see this sign above a tap or fountain, then do not drink the water.

Acqua brillante
Italian tonic water. Served in small bottles.

Acqua minerale
Mineral water. Most regions of Italy produce their own, found in the local shops and restaurants, while others are manufactured on a national and international scale.

Acqua minerale effervescente naturale
A naturally effervescent mineral water which is pleasantly bubbly. Two of the most famous brands are Ferrarelle and San Pellegrino.

Acqua minerale frizzante
Artificially gassed mineral water, where the bubbles jump out and hit you on the nose! It can sometimes have rather a salty flavour due to the carbon dioxide which is added to make it fizzy. Some of the main brands are Appia, Egeria, Nocera Umbra and San Benedetto.

Amaretto di Saronno ✪✪
One of the most popular sweet liqueurs with an almondy flavour. It is excellent drunk neat, but in the summer is also good 'on the rocks'.

Amaro ✪✪✪
Bitter-sweet liqueur made from herbs. This is one of the most characteristic types of Italian liqueur. It is recommended to aid digestion after a big meal. There are hundreds of different variations, as each region has its own, the monks being among the most avid producers. When visiting a monastery, look out for their homemade *amaro* and other liqueurs made from the ancient recipes invented by the monks.

Analcolici ✪✪✪
Non-alcoholic drinks. For once, the teetotaller need not ask for the usual tonic water, as Italy offers several of these non-alcoholic drinks as aperitifs.

Anice ✪
A dry, aniseed liqueur. Mostly used for 'splicing' black coffee.

Anisetta ✪
A strong, sweet aniseed liqueur, similar to the French Marie Brizard.

Aperol ✪✪✪

This is the trade name of an orange-coloured, bitter-sweet aperitif made from the essences of rhubarb, CHINA and gentian root. It is usually served with ice and a slice of orange with the rim of the glass dipped in sugar. Aperol is very popular due to its low alcoholic content.

Aranciata ✪
Sparkling orangeade. It is sold by the glass, bottle or can. A really fruity one is called Oransoda.

B

Bibita
A 'drink' – usually of the soft variety.

Bellini ✪✪✪
Spumante (sparkling wine) and peach juice. Originally made in Harry's Bar in Venice, but can now be found bottled.

Birra ✪
Beer. Italian beer is similar to the French beer or lager. It is pale and slightly bitter in taste, and sold in bottles and cans. Some bars and restaurants also have draught beer (*alla spina* or *spillata*).

Bitter ✪✪✪
A type of non-alcoholic aperitif. At the bar you will be asked whether you want it '*rosso o bianco*' (red or white), as there is now one with no artificial colouring which tastes as good as the original red.

Brandy ✪✪
A very palatable spirit distilled from wines. During the Fascist period, when foreign words were taboo, brandy was known as *Arzente* which, although not strictly Italian, was more acceptable than English or French! Most brandies are of a good quality and are widely drunk within Italy, even though they have never really managed to break into the international market on a very large scale.

C

Caffé ✪✪✪
Coffee. Coffee is to the Italians what tea is to the English. It is almost an offence to refuse the proffered cup when visiting friends. Coffee-making in the home, however, is a dying art as today's frenetic rythm does not allow time for the loving care with which coffee should be made. (See box below.)

Camomilla ✪
Camomile tea. This soothing drink is excellent for calming the nerves.

Campari ✪✪
Famous aperitif made from a mixture of fruit and herbs. It comes in two varieties, Bitter Campari and Campari Soda, whereas Cordial Campari is served as a liqueur.

Cappuccino ✪
Frothy milky coffee. Probably the most well-known Italian drink outside Italy, it is served with or without froth (*senza schiuma*) and often topped with a sprinkling of cocoa.

Centerbe ✪✪
A dry, 70 per cent proof, emerald-green liqueur made from herbs (the name means 100 herbs). It is worth trying, even if only to test your stamina!

China ✪
Pronounced 'keena', a bitter-tasting liqueur

A DRINK OF MANY OPTIONS

Coffee was first introduced to Europe by a 16th-century Venetian ambassador to Turkey, so it is not surprising that it became the national drink of Italy. Coffee is served in many ways and the following are some which you may encounter in addition to the familiar CAPPUCCINO and ESPRESSO.

Caffé 'al vetro' is coffee in a glass. It is a Roman fad; some can only drink their coffee when served in a glass!

Caffé coretto has been spliced with liqueur to give it an extra boost.

Caffé doppio are two servings of coffee in one.

Caffé freddo is iced coffee. A summer favourite which can also be used to make *cappuccino freddo*.

Caffé Hag (don't pronounce the 'h') is for the caffeine conscious; it is decaffeinated.

Caffé latte is a serving of coffee in a glass of hot, creamy milk.

Caffé lungo, a weaker coffee, where the barman leaves the cup under the coffee machine longer.

Caffé macchiato is 'stained' with a drop of milk.

Caffé Sport is a sweet coffee-flavoured liqueur.

Caffé valdostano, served in the traditional wooden bowl or grolla which is passed around the table, is a very intoxicating mixture of coffee, wine and GRAPPA. Served in the Valle d'Aosta in winter.

made from the bark of the Peruvian *cichona* tree. Also served hot in the winter.

Chinotto ✪✪

Italy's answer to Coke and Pepsi.

Cinzano ✪✪

Italian aperitif served with ice and a slice of lemon (see also VERMUT).

Cioccolata calda ✪✪

A thick, creamy hot chocolate topped with freshly whipped cream.

Cynar ✪

Pronounced cheenar, a bitter-tasting aperitif made from artichokes. (*Cynara* is Latin for artichoke).

D

Digestivo

A liqueur. Taken at the end of a meal, a liqueur is supposed to help the digestion.

Dolcificante

Artificial sweetener. Usually available as an alternative to sugar, at no extra charge.

E

Espresso ✪✪✪

Highly concentrated black coffee. Served in bars in small, thick-lipped cups, which keep it piping hot. It would seem to be the only thing that keeps some Italians going, judging by their frequent visits to the bar during the day! Connoisseurs say that real coffee is made only in Naples, where it is so dense that you can 'stand your spoon up in it'.

F

Fernet ✪

Bitter-tasting liqueur made from herbs and spices.

Filu Ferru ✪✪

Sardinian 'Steel Thread', a dry, 70 per cent proof liqueur only meant for the hardy! The steel thread was used to identify the buried bottles, hidden in the days of prohibition.

Frullato di frutta ✪✪✪

Fresh fruit milk shake. A meal in itself, especially when made with a *macedonia* (mixed fruit salad).

Fuoco dell'Etna ✪✪

A Sicilian bright red liqueur. It is just as powerful as the Sardinian FILU FERRU, and as warming as its name, 'Etna's fire', suggests!

G

Gazzosa ✪

A rather artificial-tasting lemonade. Good for mixing with drinks such as beer or wine.

Chatting over coffee is a way of life in Italy

Shining samples of grappa

Gingerino ✪
Non-alcoholic aperitif with a gingery taste.

Granita di caffè ✪✪✪
A coffee-flavoured water ice piled high with freshly whipped cream. Not to be missed by coffee adicts.

Granita di limone ✪✪✪
Freshly squeezed lemon juice made into ice water. Really refreshing in the hot sun.

Grappa ✪✪✪
A 50 per cent proof, colourless (golden when aged) spirit, produced mainly in the north of Italy in Piedmont and Veneto. This famous dry liqueur has been produced in Bassano del Grappa, the 'capital' of the grappa region, since the second half of the 18th century. There, near the famous bridge, the Ponte Degli Alpini, you can visit the Nardini distilleries on the banks of the river Brenta. Grappa can also be bought from family vineyards; this is often excellent and far better than some in the shops. The famous Nonino grappa can be identified by its characteristic bottles, reminiscent of the chemistry flasks in school laboratories. Some varieties contain a pear or bunch of grapes (how do they get in there?), but the grappa, although fruit-flavoured, is still dry. A sweeter version is made by adding sugar and fruit such as redcurrants or the bilberries, which are used to make the Mirtillo liqueur found in the Dolomites.

Grattachecca ✪✪✪
Crushed ice sprinkled with a fruit flavoured syrup. The *grattachecca* stalls, however, are seen very rarely nowadays but you may be lucky enough to find one at the local fair or seaside resort.

L

Latte
Milk. Italian milk is not as creamy as British. It is sold in half-litre and litre cartons and can also be bought partially skimmed (*parzialmente scremato*) or skimmed (*scremato*). The bars usually serve 'whole' milk, however, either hot (*latte caldo*), tepid (*latte tiepido*) or cold (*latte freddo*).

Latte di mandorla ✪✪
Almond milk. It is either diluted with water or mixed with other drinks and cocktails.

Latte macchiato ✪
Stained milk coloured with a dash of coffee.

Limonata ✪
Fizzy lemonade. There is a really fruity one called Lemonsoda that tastes like the real thing.

Sample Italy's unique truffle liqueur

Liquore

Liqueur. Should you be fortunate enough to be invited into an Italian home, especially in the south, you could be offered the 'family speciality', made from a recipe handed down from father to son. Home-made liqueurs are prepared for special occasions like Christmas or Easter. They are made from ingredients such as orange, lemon or tangerine peel, cherry stones, walnuts or anything else which may take the maker's fancy and is in the family tradition!

M

Mandarinetto   ✪✪
Sweet orange-flavoured liqueur. Used to give a boost to fresh fruit salad. Even better, it is heated up on on a cold day and served as a hot punch sipped through a straw; they say it works wonders for the common cold!

Martini   ✪
Probably the best known of the Italian aperitifs in all three Italian versions: dry, sweet (bianco) and rosso (see also VERMUT).

N

Nocillo   ✪✪
A medium-sweet liqueur made from Sorrento walnuts.

O

Orzata   ✪✪
A sweet but refreshing almond-flavoured barley water.

P

Punch   ✪✪✪
Pronounced 'ponch', an orange-flavoured liqueur served hot in winter.

Punt e Mes   ✪✪
One of the oldest vermouths. So-called because it was served in the bar next to the Stock Exchange in Turin, where customers were always boasting that their shares had risen a *punt e mes* (one and a half points).

R

Rabarbaro   ✪
A bitter-tasting aperitif made from rhubarb – although you would not recognise it.

S

Sambuca   ✪✪✪
A syrupy sweet aniseed liqueur. Traditionally served in Roman *trattorie* with a *mosca* (fly) floating on the top in the form of a toasted coffee bean. Sometimes it is served 'flambé' by setting light to it in the glass.

A fine selection of Tuscany wines

Sciroppo di ... ✪

Sweet syrups flavoured with fruits such as orange (*arancio*), sour cherries (*amarene*), tamarind (*tamarindo*) or mint (*menta*), diluted with mineral water to make drinks.

Seltz

Similar to soda water. Added to whisky or brandy.

Spremuta di arancio, limone e pompelmo ✪✪✪

The freshly squeezed juices of oranges, lemons and grapefruit.

Strega ✪✪

Bright yellow lemon-flavoured liqueur sold in a tall bottle with an embossed sun. Around Christmas, you can find delicious Strega-filled chocolates. Strega means 'witch'.

Succhi di frutta ✪

Italian sweetened fruit juices. They come in small bottles and in the three main flavours of peach (*pesca*), pear (*pera*) and apricot (*albicocca*). They have always been a favourite with children as they are sweeter and thicker than the citrus juices, which have been introduced to satisfy tourist demand.

T

Tè or Thè ✪

Tea. Served with lemon, unless you specifically ask for milk (*al latte*).

Tropical ✪✪

Refreshing summer drink made from almond milk mixed with syrup.

V

Vermut ✪

Vermouth. An aperitif made from wine and herbs. First made and bottled in Turin in 1786 by Signor Carpano, who founded the first distillery. Some vermouths, such as MARTINI and CINZANO, have become world famous, but there are lesser known ones made locally and called simply *Vermut*.

Vino ✪✪✪

Wine. Wine can be white (*bianco*), red (*rosso*) or rosé (*rosato*) and dry (*secco*), medium-sweet (*amabile* or *abboccato*), sweet (*dolce*) and sparkling (*frizzante*). See chapter *Wines Producing Regions* for detailed information.

Vov ✪✪

A sweet, thick, yellow-coloured liqueur made from egg yolks, sugar and alcohol. An excellent pick-me-up.

Z

Zucchero

Sugar. Sugar and artificial sweeteners are usually available on bar counters. However, in the south of Italy you will need to learn the phrase *'Senza zucchero, per favore'* if you prefer no sugar, as southern Italians tend to sweeten everything before serving and you will find drinks exceedingly sweet!

Expert wine-tasters give their opinion

Eating Out

Above: *authentic pizza baked in a wood-fired oven*
Right: *relax in a street café over lunch*

When & Where to Eat

There is a vast selection of places where you can eat out in Italy with somewhere to suit everybody's pocket and taste, from take-away pizza shops to top-class restaurants. Don't be put off by the outside appearance of a restaurant, it has little bearing on the quality of food on offer.

Italians eat out frequently; some even start their day by breakfasting with a CAPPUCCINO and CORNETTO in the bar. This is followed by mid-morning coffee, with or without an accompanying snack, and lunch in the local *trattoria* around 13.00 or 13.30 hours, unless it is possible to get home. Some prefer to return to the bar for a sandwich or to buy a slice of pizza from the nearest shop, as most office workers have only an hour for lunch.

Mid-afternoon usually means another visit to the bar for a quick coffee before going home, when they may stop on the way at the *tavola calda* (take-away) or *friggitoria* (fried food shop) to pick up something for supper.

Eating out for pleasure usually takes place in the evenings, except on Sundays, when lunch in a characteristic restaurant in the country is very common. The evening eating places range from the cheaper, less pretentious *trattoria*, *pizzeria* or *birreria* to the elegant, carpeted restaurants with their soft music and, very often, expensive menus. As a general rule, fish dishes are more expensive than meat, especially if you let yourself be tempted by the roast fish and seafood! Whatever the type of restaurant, however, VAT has always been included in the prices quoted, and the bill, usually brought only when asked for, will include cover charge (which includes bread) and service. Tipping in the region of 10 per cent is expected – unless, of course, you have been served badly. Eating places always seem to be full, whatever day of the week it is. So if you are not an early eater, it is wise to book a table, especially on Saturday evenings, unless you don't mind waiting.

One of the world's greatest settings for alfresco dining, the Rialto Bridge, Venice

Every bar or eating place closes on a fixed day every week and should display a notice saying which day this is: *Chiusura setti-manale – lunedi* (Closing day – Monday). At holiday times, this may be waived.

SNACK BAR
Bar

Bars can be found on all street corners and are part of Italian everyday life. They are places where people meet, argue, fall out, make up, put the world to rights, or simply buy the family milk. They open early in the morning at 06.00 or 06.30 hours and close in the evening any time between 21.00 hours and midnight; some even stay open until the early hours of the morning. They serve coffee and drinks of all kinds both soft and alcoholic. In the mornings, they sell freshly baked sweet rolls of all shapes and sizes, the most common being the CORNETTO, which is similar to the French croissant.

During the morning they start preparing sandwiches and rolls for lunch and often serve slices of pizza, hot dogs and hamburgers, too. Most bars have tables outside. They should all display a price list clearly indicating the difference between the prices you pay standing at the counter and those with waiter service at a table, which is more expensive – sometimes more than double. Pay at the cash till before ordering at the counter, unless you prefer to sit at a table. Hand in the receipt at the counter to get your order.

PIZZA SHOPS
Pizza a Taglio/Pizza Rustica

Pizza shops sell pizza by the 'metre'. It is made on large trays, topped with all kinds of different foods and baked in special electric ovens. It is cut into slices depending on how much you want, weighed and wrapped in paper. It can be eaten on the premises (most shops provide a few stools and cans of beer or soft drinks), consumed walking down the street, or taken home.

Many shops of this kind also make savoury rice balls (SUPPLÌ), potato or chicken croquettes, cheese dreams (*mozzarella in carrozza*) and barbecued chickens.

TAKE-AWAYS
Rosticceria/Tavola Calda

These take-aways are sometimes attached to a bar, but they also exist in their own right. They are similar to self-service restaurants where you ask for portions of the food displayed in the glass-fronted counters, then either eat it at one of the tables provided or have it wrapped to take away. They sell pasta or rice dishes, a choice of main courses and vegetables and usually offer a selection of cheese and fruit. too. Bottles of wine, beer and soft drinks are also on sale. They are a favourite place for lunch or a quick snack before going to the cinema or theatre.

FRIED FOOD SHOP
Friggitoria

As their name suggests, these shops specialise in fried food and are mainly found in the south of Italy. Here, you can buy small pizzas topped with tomato sauce (PIZZELLE), savoury doughnuts flavoured with ham, cheese or anchovy fillets, sliced vegetables dipped in batter, prawns and rings of squid, potato croquettes and many more delicacies – as long as they are fried. Like the pizza shops, they provide a few stools to enable you to enjoy your snack piping hot or, if you prefer, you can have it wrapped to take away.

LOCAL BARS
Bottiglieria/Cantina/Fiaschetteria/Trani

The original 'bottle shops' or 'flask shops' are types of very basic eating places with plain formica-topped tables and bare painted walls. Here the local senior citizens (all male) go to pass the time by playing cards, chatting and drinking the local wine, which is served in the quarter (*quartino*), half (*mezzo*) and litre measures with their characteristic seal. They

Cafés and bars are places for meeting as well as eating

sometimes serve a simple meal such as cured ham, cheese and olives but you usually have to provide your own food. For example take your own sandwiches, some ham or other snack. The name *bottiglieria* or *fiaschetteria* can sometimes be misleading, however, as nowadays some of them have been turned into ordinary *trattorie*,

ROMAN-STYLE RESTAURANTS
Cucina/Osteria/Hostaria

Some of these traditional Roman-style restaurants can be very characterful, housed in an old wine cellar with a vaulted ceiling. Others are spartan and simple, with wooden chairs and tables in a plain, white-washed room with a glass frontage separating it from the street. Whatever the setting, however, the food is usually deliciously home-made and wholesome. Prices are kept to a minimum as the tablecloths are often sheets of paper and the business is usually family-run, with sons and daughters serving at table, mother in the kitchen and father overseeing it all. This type of restaurant is usually busier at lunchtime, serving lunch to the local workmen, than in the evenings when they tend to close earlier than other establishments.

PIZZA PARLOUR
Pizzeria

Pizza restaurants are usually open only in the evenings, except for a few in large cities, which are also open at lunchtime to cater mainly for office workers and tourists. Pizza, however, is traditionally eaten in the evening and the *pizzerie* are packed with entire families, groups of young friends or couples fitting in a quick pizza before or after the cinema.

They usually open at around 19.00 hours and close around midnight (earlier in the north). Apart from pizzas and stuffed pizzas (CALZONI), they will serve savoury toasts (CROSTINI), rice balls (SUPPLÌ), potato croquettes (CROCCHETTE DI PATATE) and, on Fridays, fried fillets of cod (*filetti di baccalà*). They also usually provide other 'fillers' such as vegetables, cheese and fruit. Local wine is sold by the litre, but many Italians prefer beer with their pizza and the young drink coke or orangeade. Some *pizzerie* are also *trattorie* and, therefore, offer a full menu.

BEER-HOUSE
Birreria

These beer-houses are usually furnished in Tyrolean style, with trestle tables and benches carved in a light-coloured wood. They serve different types of draught and bottled beers, accompanied by typical south Tyrolean/Austrian dishes such as frankfurters with sauerkraut, smoked pork, goulash and mixed grills. They often serve pizza, too.

RESTAURANTS
Trattoria/Ristorante

Both names can be attributed to restaurants ranging from the more modest, cheaper ones to the extravagantly expensive ones which, by the way, are not always the best.

Trattoria usually refers to the first category and *ristorante* to the second, but often the names are interchangeable, some *ristoranti* being very simple places while some so-called *trattorie* are very fashionable restaurants. You can usually judge from the menu on display outside what kind of prices you are letting yourselves in for. Both offer a full menu from starters through to the after-dinner coffee and liqueurs, which are sometimes 'on the house'. An aperitif is usually drunk at the nearby bar while waiting for a table.

The meal begins with a starter (ANTIPASPO); many restaurants have a tempting display by the entrance to attract your attention on arrival. After the pasta, rice or soup course (*primo*) – of which you may ask for a half portion if you wish – you then move on to the fish or meat (*secondo*), depending on the restaurant's speciality. Vegetables (*contomo*) are nearly always served separately (and charged separately), unless otherwise stated. The final course (*dolce*) of either cheese, fresh fruit or a sweet completes the meal, which is accompanied by a bottle of wine or house wine served in a jug. If you do not like mineral water you can ask for a jug of tap water (*acqua semplice*). A basket of bread and bread sticks will always be brought to your table; you can ask for it to be refilled, as it is included in the cover charge.

Many Italians, nowadays, skip the main course and simply have a starter and a plate of pasta or risotto followed by vegetables or salad, or they may choose a starter instead of the meat or fish dishes. It is usually the typical 'tourist' restaurant that still frowns upon not ordering a main course. Talking about tourist restaurants, it is usually a pity to order the so-called 'Tourist Menu' (*Menu Turistico*). Unless you are very lucky, it will avoid the regional specialities and include dishes such as spaghetti with plain tomato sauce, roast chicken and chipped potatoes. It is much more interesting to order from the menu where you can try out exciting new flavours and taste combinations.

ICE-CREAM PARLOUR
Gelateria

Why not stop after the vegetable course at the restaurant and move on to a *gelateria* (ice-cream parlour) for dessert? Here you can buy ice-creams in every flavour you can think of.

They are either served in cones or small cardboard cartons for eating in the street, or in silver sundae dishes or glasses topped with a mountain of freshly whipped cream to be enjoyed while sitting at a table, with waiter service. You can also buy ice-cream by the kilo, to be taken away in special polystyrene boxes to keep it from melting. The shops stay open from late morning through to late evening, especially in the summer.

You will experience waiter service at its best in the Piazza Navona, Rome

Special Requirements

VEGETARIANS

Vegetarians, even vegans, will have no difficulty in finding sufficient variety of dishes to suit their needs. Even the most basic restaurant can offer *spaghetti al pomodoro* (spaghetti in tomato sauce) followed by some kind of substantial vegetable dish such as baked aubergines (sometimes with cheese), artichokes, peppers, green vegetables or salad, Bean dishes are common, but watch out for the ham used to flavour some regional recipes. To avoid fried foods, order fish and meat *alla griglia* (grilled) and, if you prefer, ask for it to be cooked without oil *'senza ollo, per favore'*. Boiled vegetables served with oil and lemon (*all'agro*) can always be found and fresh fruit is served in all restaurants as dessert,

Wholemeal breadsticks and bread are beginning to appear in some more fashionable restaurants and bars but are not very common. Wholemeal pasta, although readily available in shops and supermarkets, is not usually served except in vegetarian restaurants in large cities.

CHILDREN

Italians adore babies and children and tend to spoil them dreadfully. Often the magic word *bambino* will miraculously open doors, obtain favours and persuade even the most grumpy waiter to smile. Babies' bottles are heated up in bars without any problem, and baby foods can be found in all chemists (*farmacia*), grocers and supermarkets. There may not be as much choice as in Britain because Italians prefer not to use ready-made foods unless absolutely necessary. There is no age restriction in bars, and glasses of water are given freely if one of the party has ordered something. Restaurants will often produce a high-chair and can always be counted on to make *pastina in brodo* (small pasta shapes in soup) even when it is not on the menu. When sprinkled with grated cheese, this makes a filling meal, especially when followed by a slice of grilled meat or fish and fresh fruit. Half portions of most dishes can be ordered but the waiter will cheerfully bring an extra plate if you prefer to share your adult portions, although a cover charge will probably appear on the bill. *Pizzerie* are, of course, the children's favourite where they can pick the pizza up with their fingers and no-one will say anything! Eating outside is also a boon to parents as the children, once finished, can play (if it is safe and within reason) near by.

Baked aubergines, a tasty choice for vegetarians

Eating In

Above: *peppers: try them roasted as a salad*
Right: *mushrooms fresh from the market*

Shopping

As there are vitually no shopping malls in Italy, one of the greatest joys is shopping in little local stores with their wonderful personal service, and absorbing the atmosphere of the colourful street markets.

OPENING HOURS

Each region in Italy has its own laws governing the opening hours of the local shops. As a general rule, however, the food shops open early in the morning around 07.00 or 08.00 hours and close for lunch at 13.00 or 13.30 hours (in the north they close earlier at 12.00 or 12.30 hours). They reopen after the afternoon siesta at around 15.00 hours in the north and 16.30 to 17.00 hours in the centre and south. They then close in the early evening at 19.00 or 19.30 hours (earlier in the north).

The half-day closing varies from region to region but is usually Wednesday or Thursday, sometimes changing to Saturday afternoons in the summer months. The butchers' shops in some regions close on a different day to the rest, depending on their local meat deliveries. In most tourist resorts, however, at the height of the season, you usually find that the shops are open every day, including Sundays. Supermarkets are normally open all day in the big cities, or perhaps might close for an hour in the mid-afternoon.

Markets are open only in the mornings, unless a *festa* is coming up, when they will stay open through to the early evening on the day before. Cake shops stay open until later in the evening, without closing in the afternoon. They are always open on Sundays, which is their busiest day, as it is the custom in Italy when invited home for a meal to take a present of flowers, chocolates, wine or cakes. They usually close for the complete day on a Monday or Tuesday. The following is a guide to the main types of food shops you will find, the service they offer, what you can buy and when it is in season.

GROCERS' SHOPS
Alimentari/Salumeria/Salsamenteria/Pizzicheria/Norcineria

The grocers' shops look very colourful and inviting with their Parma hams, salami and sausages strung from the ceiling, their huge rounds of Parmesan cheese stacked on the shelves, their baskets of stiff, dried cod and their glass-fronted counters crammed with local cheeses and cured meats, the green and black olives and the enormous cans of tuna fish and salted anchovies. You may find your local grocers shop sign says 'Alimentari' (from *Alimenti* – foodstuffs), 'Salumeria' or 'Salsamenteria' (referring to the pork products sold), 'Pizzicheria' (from cose *pizzicanti* – things to whet the appetite) or 'Norcineria' (from the town of Norcia, home of pork butchers).

The friendly atmosphere enables you to buy just what you want; one slice of cooked ham, or 100g/4oz of cheese. The law requires the food to be weighed in or on its wrapping paper, but do not worry, the scales allow for this.

GREENGROCERS' SHOPS
Fruttivendolo/Frutteria/Frutta e Verdura/Ortaggi

Most greengrocers' shops have a display outside the shop, even if it is only two or three crates of fruit (*frutta*) or vegetables (*verdura* or *ortaggi*). Some of them, however, have a wonderful arrangement of all their produce, which is so tempting that it is difficult to choose. Everything should be priced, the prices referring to the cost per kilo, unless otherwise stated: ready prepared mixed salad or MINESTRONE for example, are sold by the *etto* (100g/4oz). There will often be piles of brown paper bags or small baskets lying around for you to serve yourself before handing everything over to the greengrocer for weighing. Some, however, do not like you to touch, especially when the soft fruits are in season.

Olives, ideal to take home as a gift

BUTCHERS' SHOPS
Macelleria/Beccheria/Carnizzeria

Most butchers' shops in towns and cities have an excellent display of large cuts of meat in their refrigerated counters. You must indicate your choice, how much you need and whether you want it sliced thinly or thickly, cut into chunks, left as a joint, pounded thin or minced. Some butchers sell ready-prepared items, such as kebabs, hamburgers and breadcrumbed veal cutlets but these are more readily obtainable at the supermarket. If you tell the butcher which dish you are planning to make, he will give you a suitable cut or suggest another with the meat available. A *macelleria equina*, by the way, is a horse meat shop!

FISHMONGERS' SHOPS
Pescheria

The fishmonger's marble slab, garnished with large green leaves, is laden with all types of fish, seafood and shellfish. The fish

Early morning at the Marsala fish market, Sicily

to be baked or grilled are weighed and sold whole but, if asked, the fishmonger will clean and descale them for you at no extra charge. The larger fish, such as swordfish or tuna, are sliced into 'steaks', and some fish, such as cod, are sometimes filleted. Get them to clean your octopus and squid, too, unless you are feeling adventurous. Shellfish is sold by the kilo; the clams come in nets which are date stamped. If any of the fish has been defrosted, a notice should say so, otherwise it should all be freshly caught.

BAKERS' SHOPS
Panificio/Fornaio/Forno/Vapoforno/ Panettiere

Each region has its own type of bread made into variously shaped loaves or rolls. You can also find home-made croissants, biscuits and cakes. Bread is bought directly from the 'oven' in small towns and villages. In large cities it is sold in grocers or 'speciality bread' shops. Bread is weighed and sold by the kilo.

CAKE SHOP
Pasticceria

Cakes are often sold in bars, and cake shops often have a counter for serving drinks.

They sell chocolates and sweets as well as large and small cakes and pastries, ice-cream cakes and ice-cream. Large cakes are weighed and sold by the kilo. Small cakes are sold individually; they can be eaten on the spot or taken away.

DAIRY
Latteria

Most supermarkets and grocers sell milk and dairy products, but bars often display the sign *Latteria*, too. They sell not only milk but cream, yoghurt and butter.

VILLAGE STORE
Generi Diversi/Emporio

In small villages, these will often be the only shop for miles around. They sell everything from shoe laces to pork chops!

MARKET
Mercato

Open-air markets, with their wooden stands and huge sun canopies, appear early in the morning in the streets and squares of most cities and towns, then pack up their stalls around lunchtime. There are also permanent covered markets in most neighbourhoods. Smaller villages have travelling markets which visit one day a week. They are all usually excellent for both value and freshness. There is a feeling of bustle and activity, with the stallholders crying out their wares in local dialect. The fruit and vegetables are a wonderful sight. Whatever is in season is heaped on to stalls and arranged so temptingly that you usually buy far more than you intended!

Chillies, not only a mainstay of Italian cooking, but an attractive decoration hung in the kitchen

STREET STALL
Bancarella

Found along the roadside, often rigged up in the back of a lorry, they often sell just one item – whatever happens to be in season, such as strawberries or artichokes.

FROZEN FOODS
Surgelati

These stores specialise in everything frozen, from cuts of meat and whole fish down to ice-cream. You will not find complete ready-made frozen meals, however.

Fresh produce is delivered early in the morning

Recipes

Here are a few recipes for you to 'cook Italian' while on holiday or to try out back home. The easily made dishes are marked ✪ and the more time-consuming ones are marked ✪✪. It would be worthwhile looking to see whether you could buy some of the essential ingredients while you are in the country.

MINESTRONE

THICK VEGETABLE SOUP
✪

SERVES FOUR

Tastier when made the day, or morning, before.

1 thick slice lean 'steaky' bacon
1 large clove garlic, skinned
olive oil
500g/1lb roughly chopped mixed vegetables, such as carrots, celery, leeks, cabbage, cauliflower, courgettes, spinach, broccoli
2 ripe tomatoes, roughly chopped
2 medium potatoes, peeled and diced
salt
100g/3½oz *tubetti* (small, short pasta tubes)
75g/3oz Parmesan cheese, grated, to serve

Chop the bacon into small pieces. Cut the garlic clove into 3 to 4 pieces. Coat the bottom of a deep, thick-bottomed saucepan with olive oil, add the garlic and bacon and fry until the garlic is golden and the bacon crisp. Add all the chopped vegetables. Cover with water, add salt to taste and simmer for about 40 minutes until the vegetables have become a thickish soup. Add a little water to prevent the soup from becoming too thick while cooking the pasta. Bring back to the boil, add the pasta and cook until it is *al dante*. Serve the soup in individual bowls with grated Parmesan cheese.

Antipasto all'italiana

ANTIPASTO ALL'ITALIANA

ITALIAN–STYLE STARTER
✪

SERVES SIX TO EIGHT AS A STARTER

8 anchovy fillets (1 small can)
4 individuai portions butter
100g/3½oz green olives
200g/7oz thinly sliced cured ham (*prosciutto crudo*)
200g/1oz sliced mixed salami
1 small jar mixed pickles
4 small wild boar sausages (*salsicce di cinghiale*)

Drain the oil from the anchovy fillets and roll up each one. Cut the portions of butter into halves and top each with an anchovy roll. Arrange the sliced meats attractively on a platter, putting the olives, pickles, sausages and anchovies in the middle (or make individual arrangements on plates). Serve with crusty bread or breadsticks.

BRUSCHETTA CON POMODORI

GARLIC BREAD WITH TOMATOES
✪

SERVES FOUR

This garlic bread can also be served with sliced ham.

4 medium-ripe tomatoes, finely chopped
8–10 fresh basil leaves
4 tablespoons olive oil
salt
4 large thick slices crusty bread
1 clove garlic

Place the tomatoes in a bowl. Wash and pat dry the basil leaves, discarding the stalks. Tear the leaves into small pieces and add them to the tomatoes with the olive oil. Add salt to taste.

Toast the bread over a wood/charcoal fire (or under the grill) until browned on both sides. Half-peel the garlic and rub it over one side of each piece of toast. Cut the slices of toast in half and top each piece with the tomato imxture. Serve immediately.

SPAGHETTI AGLIO, OLIO, PEPERONCINO

SPAGHETTI WITH OIL, GARLIC AND CHILLI
✪

SERVES FOUR

This simple but tasty dish, which can be made in minutes, is a favourite with Italians late at night, after the cinema or even at the end of a wedding feast!

400g/14oz spaghetti
1 glass olive oil (about a wine glass, or more)
4 cloves garlic, skinned and finely chopped
1 dried red chilli, crushed
1 tablespoon roughly chopped fresh parsley (optional)

Cook the spaghetti in a pan of boiling salted water. Heat the oil in a small frying pan and add the garlic and chilli. Fry over a low heat so that the garlic becomes crunchy.

When the spaghetti is *al dente*, drain well and mix with the oil and garlic. Serve immediately, sprinkled with chopped parsley, if using.

BUCATINI ALL'AMATRICANA

BUCATINI AMATRICE STYLE
✪

SERVES FOUR

Amatrice, which gives its name to this sauce, is a small mountain town about 60km (37 miles) northeast of Rome.

1 (400g/ l4oz) can finely chopped plum tomatoes
olive oil
1 small chilli
1 small onion, skinned and chopped
2 thick slices lean streaky bacon (pancetta)
2 teaspoons concentrated tomato purée
salt
400g/l4oz bucatini
25g/3oz pecorino cheese, grated

Liquidise the tomatoes or crush them with a fork. Coat the base of a deep heavy-based frying pan with olive oil. Add the chilli crushing it to release its flavour. Add the onion and bacon and fry until the onion is transparent and the bacon crisp. Add the tomato purée, tomatoes and salt to taste, and cook over a low heat, stirring occasionally, for about 30 minutes until the sauce becomes thick.

Meanwhile, bring a pan of salted water to the boil for the *bucatini* and cook the pasta so that it is ready at the same time as the sauce. Drain the pasta well, transfer to a warmed serving dish and mix with half the grated cheese and the sauce. Serve, with the rest of the grated cheese to be added as desired.

Bucatini all'amatricana – bucantini *are thick spaghetti*

IMPEPATA DI COZZE

PEPPERED MUSSELS
✪

SERVES FOUR AS A LIGHT MEAL, SIX TO EIGHT AS
A STARTER

*This is obviously best made with mussels
you have just caught yourself! However,
fresh mussels are readily available from all
fishmongers in Italy. This recipe is not
suitable for frozen or bottled ones.*

1.5kg/31b fresh mussels
freshly ground black pepper
2 large lemons

Clean the mussels really well by putting
them in a large bowl or bucket of water
(seawater if available) and rubbing the shells
together to remove seaweed or other
foreign bodies encrusted on them. Pull away
the beard or seaweed-like strands from each
mussel and discard. Rinse well and place in
a large covered pan over a high heat, tossing
them frequently until the shells have all
opened. Do not leave them over the heat
longer than necessary or the mussels will
overcook. Discard any mussels that do not
open.

Using a draining spoon, place all the
mussels in a large serving bowl. Filter the
cooking liquor if necessary to remove any
sand, then pour it hot over the mussels.
Sprinkle very generously with the black
pepper and serve with wedges of lemon and
chunks of crusty bread. Use the shells to eat
the mussels, scooping up a little juice with
each, and squeezing a little lemon on to the
mussel before eating.

PASTA AL FORNO

BAKED PASTA
✪✪

SERVES FOUR

*Half-litre cartons of white sauce (béchamel)
can be bought in most Italian grocers' shops
and supermarkets.*

100g/3½oz butter or margarine
200g/7oz mushrooms, thinly sliced
1 clove garlic, skinned
200g/7oz small frozen peas
2 thick slices lean cooked ham, chopped,
**   fat removed**
300g/10oz *rigatoni*
0.5litre/1 pint pouring white sauce
**   (béchamel)**
100g/3oz Parmesan cheese, grated
salt and pepper

Melt a third of the butter in a pan and fry the
mushrooms with the garlic clove. Remove
the garlic and discard. Cook the peas in
boiling salted water. Drain and add to the
mushrooms with the ham. Cook the *rigatoni*
in a pan of boiling salted water until three-
quarters cooked, then drain.

Set the oven at 200°C, 400°F, gas 6. Heat
the white sauce, add half the grated cheese
and another third of the butter. Mix two-
thirds of the sauce with the *rigatoni*. Layer
the *rigatoni* with the peas, ham and
mushrooms in an ovenproof dish (or
disposable foil baking tin), finishing with a
layer of pasta.

Pour the rest of the sauce over the top,
sprinkle with the rest of the grated cheese
and flakes of butter. Bake at the top of the
oven for 15 to 20 minutes until golden
brown. Serve with a green salad. This makes
a filling one-course meal.

BRASATO AL BAROLO

BRAISED BEEF IN BAROLO WINE
✪✪

SERVES SIX

750g/1lb 10oz lean beef
50g/2oz lean streaky bacon
1 medium onion, skinned and sliced
1 large carrot, peeled and sliced
1 stick celery, sliced rosemary, 2 cloves, 1 clove garlic. 1 bay leaf and 2–3 peppercorns tied in a muslin bag
1 bottle of Barolo wine flour
50g/2oz butter
salt and pepper
small glass brandy
cornflour, if necessary

Lard the meat with half the bacon. Finely chop the remaining bacon. Put the meat in a deep bowl with the onion, carrot, celery and the herb and spice bag. Pour the wine over the meat, cover and leave to marinate in a cool place overnight.

Remove the meat, pat dry and roll in flour. Melt the butter in a flameproof casserole, fry the chopped bacon and brown the meat well on all sides. Pour in the brandy and cook for a minute or so. Add the marinade. When it comes to the boil, cook for 15 minutes before removing the spices. Season to taste, cover and braise over a low heat for 2 to 3 hours.

Remove the meat and keep warm. Liquidise the sauce, then bring it back to the boil and thicken with a little blended cornflour, if necessary. Adjust for salt. Thinly slice the meat and serve, coated with the sauce, on a warmed platter, with potato purée or POLENTA.

PASTA E FAGIOLI ALLA MARUZZARA

PASTA AND BEANS IN TOMATO SAUCE
✪

SERVES FOUR

A simple dish combining two of the staples of the Italian diet. Excellent for vegetarians.

100g/3½oz canned plum tomatoes
2 cloves garlic, skinned
olive oil
1 teaspoon crushed oregano
salt
2 (400g/14oz) cans cannellini beans
250g/8oz mixed pasta (*pasta mista*)

Liquidise or crush the tomatoes. Cut the garlic cloves into 3 to 4 pieces. Coat the base of a thick-bottomed saucepan with olive oil and fry the garlic until golden. Add the tomatoes, oregano and salt to taste, then cook for 5 to 6 minutes. Drain the beans, mix them with the tomato sauce adding a glass of water, and heat through.

Meanwhile, cook the pasta in a pan of boiling salted water until *al dente*, Drain and mix with the beans and tomato sauce. Serve in warmed individual terracotta dishes.

POLPI AFFOGATI

DROWNED OCTOPUS
✪✪

SERVES FOUR

This dish is well worth the effort if you have been snorkeling and happen to have caught your own octopus. Otherwise, it can be made back home.

4 small octopus, about 200g/7oz each
1 (400g/14oz) can plum tomatoes
2 cloves garlic, skinned
olive oil
1 hot chilli
1 tablespoon fresh parsley, roughly
   chopped

To clean the octopus, turn the heads inside out and remove the ink sacks (be careful of the ink). Remove the eyes and hard 'beaks' in the middle of the tentacles, Rinse well, making sure that there is no sand stuck to the suction pads. Liquidise or crush the tomatoes and slice the garlic cloves. Coat the base of a deep frying pan with olive oil, add the chilli, crushing it to release the flavour. Add the garlic and fry until golden. Add the octopus, cover and cook, turning it occasionally, until tender (about 30 minutes). Add the tomatoes and cook for a further 10 to 15 minutes until the sauce becomes thick. Taste for salt, but it is not usually needed. Serve sprinkled generously with chopped parsley.

TRENETTE AL PESTO

'FLATTENED' SPAGHETTI WITH FRESH BASIL PASTE
✪

SERVES FOUR

This is perhaps best made in your food processor at home, but it would be a shame not to try the 'chopped' version. The fresh Italian basil is too good to miss. Don't forget to take a packet of pine kernels home.

2 large bunches fresh basil
2–3 mint leaves (not necessary with
   Ligurian basil)
2 cloves garlic, skinned

1 tablespoon pine kernels
75g/3oz pecorino cheese, grated
about 2/3 wine glass olive oil
400g/ l4oz *trenette* or *linguine*

Wash and pat dry the basil leaves, discarding the stalks. Finely chop together the basil, mint, garlic and pine kernels either on a chopping board or in a food processor, adding part of the grated cheese as you chop. Transfer the chopped ingredients to a bowl and slowly beat in the oil and the rest of the cheese until a thick, creamy paste is obtained

Meanwhile, cook the pasta in a pan of boiling salted water until *al dente*. Drain, keeping a cup of pasta water. Mix the pasta and pesto together, adding enough pasta water to make a creamy sauce which coats the pasta. Serve immediately.

Ingredients for pesto, *a classic Italian sauce*

RISOTTO AI FUNGHI PORCINI

MUSHROOM RISOTTO
✪✪

SERVES FOUR

Packets of dried porcim *(edible boletus mushrooms) can be found in all Italian grocers and supermarkets.*

25g/1oz packet of dried *porcini*
olive oil
1 small onion, skinned and finely chopped
300g/10oz risotto rice
1 glass dry white wine about 1 litre/2 pints boiling meat stock
knob of butter or margarine
75g/3oz Parmesan cheese, grated

Cover the *porcini* with a little boiling water and leave to soak for about 30 minutes, then squeeze out gently and roughly chop. Reserve a tablespoon of the liquid. Coat the base of a shallow saucepan with olive oil and fry the onion until transparent. Add the rice. As soon as it has absorbed the oil, add the wine. As soon as this has been absorbed, stirring all the time, start adding the boiling stock, just enough to cover the rice. Allow the rice to absorb it before adding more. When the rice is half cooked, add the *porcini* and reserved liquid. The risotto is ready when the rice is just cooked through and is neither too dry nor too liquid. Stir in the knob of butter and a third of the grated cheese. Allow to melt into the risotto before serving with the rest of the cheese, to be added as desired.

Good risotto is moist and creamy

SALTIMBOCCA ALLA ROMANA

ROMAN 'JUMP-IN-MOUTHS'
✪

SERVES FOUR

8 small thin slices veal
salt and pepper
8 small sage leaves
4 slices Parma ham, halved
butter or olive oil for frying
1 glass dry white wine

Trim the fat off the veal. Lightly season the slices and place a sage leaf on the centre of each. Top each slice of veal with half a slice of ham and secure with a wooden cocktail stick. Fry the slices in butter or olive oil over a high heat until cooked. Add the wine and continue cooking until the sauce becomes thick. Serve immediately, pouring the sauce over the escalopes.

PENNE ALL'ARRABBIATA

'FURIOUS' QUILS
✪

SERVES FOUR

olive oil
2 cloves garlic, skinned
2 hot chillies, crushed
1 (400g/14oz) can plum tomatoes
salt
400g/14oz *penne* (pasta quills)
1 heaped tablespoon roughly chopped fresh parsley

Coat the base of a thick-bottomed frying pan with olive oil and fry the garlic and crushed chillies. Liquidise or crush the tomatoes.

When the garlic is golden, add the tomatoes and salt to taste. Cook for 10 to 15 minutes until the sauce becomes thicker. Meanwhile, cook the pasta in a pan of boiling salted water until *al dente*. Drain well and mix with the sauce. Sprinkle generously with chopped parsley.

RIGATONI ALLA PIZZAIOLA

RIGATONI, PIZZA-MAKER STYLE
✪

SERVES FOUR

The meat is delicious served with chipped potatoes as a main course.

1½ (400g/14oz) cans plum tomatoes
3 cloves garlic, skinned
olive oil
1 teaspoon crushed oregano
4 slices lean beef (or 4 thin steaks)
salt
400g/14oz *rigatoni*
75g/3oz Parmesan cheese, grated, to serve

Liquidise or crush the tomatoes. Cut the garlic cloves into 3 to 4 pieces. Coat the base of a deep thick-bottomed frying pan with olive oil, add the tomatoes, garlic, oregano, beef and salt to taste. Simmer over a low heat, stirring occasionally, for about 30 minutes until the sauce becomes thicker and darker.

Meanwhile, cook the *rigatoni* in a pan of salted water so that the pasta will be cooked *al dente* just as the sauce is ready. Drain well and mix with the sauce, leaving the meat for the main course. Serve with grated Parmesan cheese.

COSTOLETTA ALLA MILANESE

BONELESS MILANESE CUTLETS

SERVES FOUR

These golden fried cutlets are similar to Wiener Schnitzel. The butcher will flatten the meat for you if you ask.

2 small eggs (size 6)
salt
grated rind of ½ lemon
1 small packet toasted breadcrumbs
4 large thin slices lean veal or young beef
butter, margarine or olive oil, for frying
1 large lemon, cut into wedges

Break the eggs into a dish and beat well, adding salt and the lemon rind. Put a pile of breadcrumbs on to a sheet of greaseproof paper next to the dish.

Remove any fat from the meat and pound thinly with a meat-mallet. Cut each slice in two. Coat with egg and breadcrumbs, pressing them well on to the meat with the palms of your hands. Fry until golden. Serve piping hot with the lemon wedges.

FEGATO ALLA VENEZIANA

VENETIAN–STYLE LIVER

SERVES FOUR

Venice's best known dish.

2 large onions, skinned
olive oil
600g/1¼1b calves' liver, sliced

salt and pepper
1 small glass dry white wine

Finely slice the onions lengthways. Coat the base of a thick-bottomed frying pan with olive oil, add the onions, cover and cook until transparent, stirring occasionally to prevent burning. Cut the liver into short, thin strips, season and add to the onions. Cook over a high heat, stirring all the time, until the liver is almost cooked, Add the wine and cook until the sauce becomes thick. Serve immediately with potato purée or POLENTA.

PISELLI AL PROSCIUTTO

HAM–FLAVOURED PEAS

SERVES FOUR

These peas are also delicious mixed with pasta as a first course. Bacon can be used instead of Parma ham.

1 thick slice Parnia ham, about 100g/3½oz
olive oil
1 medium onion, skinned and finely chopped
450g/14½oz packet small frozen peas (petits pois)
salt

Chop the ham into small pieces. Coat the bottom of a wide saucepan or large frying pan with olive oil. Heal the oil, then fry the onion until transparent, adding the ham after about 5 to 7 minutes. Add the peas and stir in just enough water to cover. Add salt to taste and bring to the boil. Reduce the heat, if necessary, and simmer until the peas are tender, and most of the liquid has evaporated. Serve hot or warm.

MELANZANE ALLA PARMIGIANA

AUBERGINES, PARMA STYLE
⊛⊛

SERVES FOUR

A filling one-course meal.

**800g/1¾1b small, firm aubergines
coarse-grained cooking salt
olive oil
8–10 fresh basil leaves
500g/1lb mozzarella cheese
1 (400g/14oz) can plum tomatoes
salt and pepper
100g/3½oz Parmesan cheese,
  grated**

Ingredients for Melanzine alla parmigiana, *a favourite summer dish*

Rinse, dry and cut the aubergines lengthways into slices about 0.25cm/⅛ inch thick. Layer them in a colander, sprinkling a little cooking salt between each layer. Place a weight (a deep saucepan full of water is ideal) on top and leave for about 1 hour for the salt to bring out the bitter juices. Rinse the aubergines under cold running water and squeeze well. Fry the slices in olive oil until browned on each side. Drain well on kitchen paper. Set the oven at 200°C, 400°F, gas 6. Tear the basil leaves into small pieces. Cut the mozzarella into thin slices. Liquidise or crush the tomatoes, seasoning them slightly. Spread a little of the tomatoes over the base of an ovenproof dish. Cover with a layer of aubergines, followed by a little more tomato, a few torn basil leaves, half the mozzarella and sprinkle half the grated Parmesan on top. Repeat, using up all the ingredients. Bake in the oven for about 30 minutes until golden on top. Serve warm or cold.

FRITTATA DI ZUCCHINI

COURGETTE OMELETTE

SERVES FOUR

4 large eggs (size 1)
50g/2oz Parmesan cheese, grated
salt and pepper olive oil
1 medium onion, skinned and chopped
6 smallish courgettes, thinly sliced

Beat the eggs with the cheese, salt and pepper. Heat a little olive oil in a large non–stick frying pan and fry the onion. Add the courgettes and cook until just tender. Cover the vegetables with the egg mixture and cook over a low heat, without stirring, until set and golden underneath. Slide the omelette on to a large plate, turn the frying pan upside down and place it over the *frittata*. Holding the plate carefully, rapidly turn the frying pan over and cook the *frittata* on the other side. Serve hot or cold.

Italian-style omelette

MOZZARELLA IN CARROZZA

'MOZZARELLA IN COACHES'

SERVES FOUR

The bread is best if not fresh. Make sure the slices are not too dissimilar from the size of the mozzarella slices.

2 large eggs (size 1)
salt and pepper
8 small thin slices bread
4 slices mozzarella cheese about
 1cm/½inch thick
olive oil

Beat the eggs and salt and pepper to taste in a shallow bowl. Remove the bread crusts and make 'sandwiches' with the mozzarella. Dip them in the beaten egg, making sure that the bread is soaked with egg. Fry in olive oil until crisp and golden on both sides. Drain well on kitchen paper and serve piping hot,

PIZZELLE

SMALL FRIED PIZZAS
✪✪

SERVES SIX

These are a real treat for the children as they are eaten in the fingers. Without the sauce, sprinkled with sugar and cinnamon, they also make a good dessert.

40g/1½oz fresh yeast
550ml/18fl oz tepid water (about 3 glasses)
700g/1½1b plain flour
1 teaspoon salt
1 (800g/1lb12oz) can plum tomatoes
3 large cloves garlic, skinned
8–10 fresh basil leaves
olive oil
salt
oil for deep frying
100g/3½oz Parmesan cheese, grated, to serve

Dissolve the yeast in a little of the tepid water. Sift the flour and salt into a large bowl, making a well in the centre. Add the yeast and all the water. Mix together to form a soft, sticky dough. Turn out on to a well floured surface and knead for about 10 minutes, adding more flour if necessary, until the dough becomes soft and elastic. Shape into a long thin roll and cut into 24 pieces. Roll each piece into a small ball and put them on to a floured board. Cover and leave in a warm place to rise for about 1 hour.

Meanwhile, prepare the sauce. Liquidise or crush the tomatoes. Cut the garlic cloves into 3 to 4 pieces. Tear the basil leaves into small pieces. Coat the base of a thick-bottomed frying pan with olive oil and fry the garlic until golden. Add the tomatoes, half the basil leaves and salt to taste. Cook for about 15 minutes until the sauce becomes thicker. Turn off the heat and add the rest of the basil. When the *pizzelle* have doubled in size, flatten them into rounds, pulling them into shape with your fingers. Deep fry them, two or three at a time, depending on the size of the pan, until they float and are golden. Stack them on a serving plate, keeping them warm, and serve topped with the tomato sauce and grated Parmesan cheese.

TONNO E FAGIOLI

TUNA AND BEANS
✪

SERVES SIX

A favourite starter in Italian restaurants abroad, this is substantial enough to serve for a light lunch.

1 red-skinned onion, skinned and thinly sliced
2 (400g/14oz) cans cannellini beans
2 (160g/5oz) cans tuna, flaked
olive oil
salt and pepper
juice of 1 lemon
1 tablespoon fresh parsley, roughly chopped

Leave the onion to soak a while in cold water. Drain the beans and empty them into a serving bowl. Add the skinned onion and tuna, then dress with olive oil, salt to taste and sprinkle generously with pepper. Add the lemon juice and mix lightly, taking care not to break the beans. Serve chilled, sprinkled with parsley and accompanied by chunks of crusty bread.

113

PANZANELLA

SERVES FOUR

This refreshing snack is sometimes eaten for breakfast in the summer, particularly in the south.

6 large ripe tomatoes
salt
8–10 fresh basil leaves
4 *freselle* large ring-shaped rusks)
1 small red-skinned onion, skinned and thinly sliced olive oil

Roughly chop the tomatoes, adding salt to taste. Tear the basil leaves into small pieces. Dip the rusks in cold water, then place on individual plates. Top them with the tomatoes and onion, sprinkle generously with olive oil and basil. Eat while still crunchy, or allow to soak a little in the juices.

INSALATA CAPRESE

CAPRI SALAD

SERVES FOUR

4 large tomatoes
800g/1¾lb mozzarella cheese
10–12 fresh basil leaves
olive oil
salt and pepper

Thinly slice the tomatoes. Cut the mozzarella into slices, about lcm/½inch thick. Arrange them both on a serving platter. Tear the basil leaves into small pieces and use to garnish the tomatoes and mozzarella. Sprinkle with olive oil and serve immediately, everyone seasoning their own portion

Rice salad, a variable feast

INSALATA DI RISO

RICE SALAD

SERVES FOUR TO SIX

You can vary the ingredients to your liking in this tasty dish. It makes a refreshing change from sandwiches for picnics.

400g/14oz long-grain rice
100g/3½ mild cheese
10 black olives
2 small frankfurters (*wurstel*)
6 medium gherkins
2 large tomatoes
2 hard-boiled eggs
1 (160g/5oz) can tuna, drained and flaked
juice of 1 large lemon
2 tablespoons olive oil
salt and pepper

Cook the rice in a pan of boiling water until *al dente*. Drain well and chill in the refrigerator. Dice the cheese, stone and roughly chop the olives, cut the frankfurters and gherkins into thin slices and roughly chop the tomatoes and hard-boiled eggs, Put all the ingredients, with the tuna, into a large bowl and add the rice and lemon juice. Mix well, adding the oil, and season to taste. Chill before serving.

PEPERONI ARROSTITI

ROASTED PEPPER SALAD

SERVES FOUR

3 large red or yellow peppers
1 tablespoon olive oil
salt
2 cloves garlic, skinned and chopped
1½ teaspoons crushed oregano

Wash and dry the peppers, leaving them whole, and place them on a sheet of foil under the grill. Cook, turning them over frequently, until the skin has charred and come away from the flesh. Allow to cool a little (but not become cold) before skinning them with your fingers. Remove the stalks and seeds, then tear the flesh lengthways into thin strips. Dress the pepper strips with oil, salt, garlic and oregano. Combine well and leave to cool before serving

PESCHE AL VINO

PEACHES IN WINE

SERVES FOUR

6 large peaches
1½ tablespoons caster sugar
dry white or red wine

Skin, stone and cut the peaches into thin slices. Place them in a serving dish and add the sugar. Cover with wine and leave to marinate in the refrigerator, preferably for several hours. Serve chilled.

ZABAIONE AL MARSALA

MARSALA-FLAVOURED EGG FLIP
✪✪

SERVES FOUR

Cream sherry makes a good substitute for Marsala.

4 egg yolks
4 tablespoons caster sugar
8 egg shells of Marsala wine
sponge fingers for dipping

Whisk the egg yolks and sugar in a bowl until thick and foamy. Place the bowl over a pan of boiling water and, while still whisking, slowly add the Marsala, a shellful at a time. Continue whisking until the mixture is thick, light and creamy. Never let the mixture boil or it will curdle. Serve hot or cold in long-stemmed wine glasses with sponge fingers

TIRAMISÙ

PICK-ME-UP
✪✪

SERVES SIX

Double cream can be substituted for the mascarpone.

3 eggs, separated
300g/10oz caster sugar
300g/10oz *mascarpone*
1 small glass brandy
200g/7oz sponge fingers (*savoiardi*)
1 teacup strong black coffee, slightly sweetened
1 tablespoon cocoa powder

Whisk the egg yolks with the sugar in a bowl until thick, pale and creamy. Add the *mascarpone* and brandy and continue whisking until well mixed. Whisk the egg whites until they form stiff peaks and gently fold them into the mixture.

In a shallow serving dish, layer the creamy mixture with the sponge fingers quickly dipped in coffee, finishing with a layer of creamy mixture. Chill in the refrigerator for several hours. Serve thickly dredged with cocoa.

Zabaione, a popular dessert

Practical
Information

Above: *market day in the ancient city of L'Aquila*
Right: *octopus, popular throughout Italy*

SELF CATERING

Most self-catering apartments are well equipped with modern cookers and refrigerators, and they will have saucepans, coffee percolators, cutlery, plates and glasses. Disposable plastic plates and cups can be bought in packs of 50s or 100s in most shops and supermarkets. They are well worth the small, extra cost! Choose dishes that are quick and easy to prepare and cook. You might consider taking a few convenience foods with you, particularly any favourites that are not available in Italy. The water is drinkable and can safely be used for making ice-cubes.

MINOR ILLNESSES

Boiled rice mixed with a little olive oil and grated Parmesan cheese is a favourite with Italians when not feeling too well. Squeezed lemon juice is also excellent for stopping diarrhoea. When having to eat out, ask to eat *in bianco* (without sauces/plain) with everything grilled, poached or boiled.

LAWS/REGULATIONS

By law you should always make sure that you are given an official fiscal receipt (*ricevuta fiscale*) in restaurants, in case of spot checks by the Finance Police. The same applies to the receipt from the cash till in shops and bars. However, common practice is not always as strict with regard to providing receipts.

TIGHT BUDGET

Buy a good supply of dried and canned foods from the nearest supermarket, as these can cost quite a bit more in the village stores or local grocer's shop. Markets are best for freshness and cheapness when buying fruit and vegetables, although roadside stalls can also offer bargains if you are buying in large quantities. Fish can be picked up cheaply in the markets at closing time, if you are prepared to take whatever is left. It is often sold off at as little as half price. Remember that white fish is twice as expensive as meat, but oily fish such as anchovies and mackerel are much cheaper. Bottles of wine and liqueurs are, again, usually cheaper at supermarkets but, of course, some special locally made wines and liqueurs are only available at source.

The cheapest eating place is often the unpretentious *trattoila* on the corner where you can get a full, wholesome meal quite inexpensively if you do not mind not having much choice. *The pizza a taglio* shops provide slices of pizza for economical, filling snacks, while in the *tavola calda/rosticceria* you can choose just a salad, if that is all you want. When eating out in restaurants, *pizzerie* and *trattorie*, always check the menu on display before entering, to see what kind of prices you are letting yourself in for!

The euro is the official currency of Italy. Euro bank notes and coins were introduced on 1st January 2002. Bank notes are in denominations of 5, 10, 20, 50, 100, 200 and 500 euros and coins are in denominations of 1, 2, 5, 10, 20 and 50 cents and 1 and 2 euros.

Euro travellers' cheques are widely accepted as well as all major credit cards.

SPECIAL EVENTS

Christmas Italians tend to spend Christmas with the family, starting with an enormous dinner on Christmas Eve finishing just in time for everyone to go to Midnight Mass. The menu is traditionally based on fish and vegetable dishes followed by an incredible selection of fresh fruit, nuts, dried fruits and the traditional Christmas cakes, PANETTONE or PANDORO, not to mention all the regional Christmas specialities. Lunch on Christmas day is served later than usual, starting with stuffed pasta in consommé followed by a roast (often turkey nowadays), potatoes, vegetables and, once again, a selection of fruit, nuts and cakes.

New Year New Year's Eve means another enormous dinner, this time lasting through into the New Year. In the home it is often fish based but the restaurants really go to town inventing the most incredible menus comprising starters, two or three first courses, fish, meat, game, vegetables, fruit, dessert and, after midnight, sliced, boiled sausage with lentils to guarantee wealth in the coming year!

Carnevale Not to be confused with carnivals, *carnevale* is the period before Lent, from the Thursday up until the Tuesday before Ash Wednesday. Cakes such as CHIACCHIRE, FRAPPE and CASTAGNOLE are traditionally served at the various fancy dress parties that take place during *carnevale* time. Some regions also have special rich dishes, such as LASAGNE ALLA NAPOLETANA, which is a much enjoyed treat before the privations of Lent.

Easter Chocolate Easter eggs of all sizes, from the tiny filled ones sold by the *etto* (100g/4oz) to the gigantic ones raffled off in bars, appear all over Italy soon after *carnevale*. They all have a surprise hidden in the centre, which can be anything from a plastic monster to good quality costume jewellery, depending on the price. Easter Sunday lunch traditionally starts with salami and hard-boiled eggs, followed by freshly made stuffed pasta in a sauce or consommé and roast lamb or goat. The COLOMBA is a special Easter cake found everywhere, along with regional special-ities such as PIZZA DI PASQUA from Umbria, TORTA PASQUALINA from Liguria and PASTIERA NAPOLETANA.

Festa Days *Festa* are religious celebrations. Some *festa* days have special cakes, such as BIGNÉ DI SAN GIUSEPPE on St Joseph's day. Look out for regional saints' days. Villages and towns always have a fair with street stalls selling regional specialities, toasted nuts, olives and candy floss to celebrate their patron saint.

Sagre Look out for the local Sagra del..., a festival to celebrate the harvesting of certain fruit and vegetables, or the making of wine or sausages. They often take place at weekends and the whole village takes part in the making and selling of local dishes and products made from the foodstuff in question. Grapes, artichokes, wine, truffles, chestnuts, cherries and sausages are just a few examples.

SHOPPING BASKET

The average price of items found in a typical family food basket is likely to be as follows

- ✪ Bread €1.1
- ✪ Wine €2.6
- ✪ Cornflakes €2.1
- ✪ Milk 1 litre €0.8
- ✪ Apples 1 kilo €1.1
- ✪ Cooked meat (ham) 250 grams €4.7
- ✪ Cheese 500 grams €5.2
- ✪ 6 eggs €0.7

CUSTOMS

YES
From another EU country for personal use (guidelines):
800 cigarettes, 200 cigars, 1 kilogram of tobacco
10 litres of spirits (over 22%)
20 litres of aperitifs
90 litres of wine, of which 60 litres can be sparkling wine
110 litres of beer

From a non-EU country for your personal use, the allowances are:
200 cigarettes OR
50 cigars OR 250 grams of tobacco
1 litre of spirits (over 22%)
2 litres of intermediary products (e.g. sherry) and sparkling wine
2 litres of still wine
50 grams of perfume
0.25 litres of eau de toilette
The value limit for goods is 175 euros.

Travellers under 17 years of age are not entitled to the tobacco and alcohol allowances.

NO
Drugs, firearms, ammunition, offensive weapons, obscene material, unlicensed animals.

USEFUL WORDS AND PHRASES

PRONUNCIATION

- ✪ The imitated pronunciation should read as if it were English, bearing in the mind the following main points.

- ✪ Accentuating the correct syllable is very important in Italian. Stress tends to be on the last syllable but one, eg fratello = frah**tay**llo; ragazza = rah**gah**tzah.

- ✪ a is like a in car, eg pasta = pah**stah**; e is like ay in way, eg sera = sayrah; i is like ee in meet, eg vini = veenee; o is like o in not, eg notte = nottay; u is like oo in foot, eg uno = oono.

- ✪ g before e and i is like j in jet, eg giro = jeero; elsewhere it is like g in go, eg gatto = gahtto; gn is like ni in onion, eg bagbo = bahneeo.

- ✪ r is always strongly pronounced – children imitating an electric buzzer with the tip of their tongue come close, eg buon giorno.

- ✪ c before e and i is like ch in chip, eg cinema = cheenaymah; elsewhere it is like c in cat, eg casa = kahzah; ch is like c in cat, eg chi = kee.

- ✪ The letter h is always silent, but can modify the sound of of letters c and g.

- ✪ Double consonants in Italian are pronounced by lingering on the first of the two consonants, eq mamma = mam-ma).

HOW TO ASK A QUESTION

- ✪ **Which one...?** Quale...? kwahlay?

- ✪ **Why...?** Perchè...? pakrkay?

- ✪ **When...?** Quando...? kwahndo?

- ✪ **Who...?** Chi...? kee?

- ✪ **What...?** Che (cosa)...? kay (kosah)?

- ✪ **Where are you from?** Da dove viene? dah dovay veeayhnay?

- ✪ **Where...?** Dove...? dovay?

- ✪ **Do you know...?** Saprebbe...? saprebbay?

- ✪ **How far is that...?** Quanto è lontano...? kwahnto ay lontahno?

- ✪ **How much...?** Quanto...? kwahnto?

- ✪ **How...?** Come...? komay?

- ✪ **Could you...?** Potrebbe...? potraybbay?

- ✪ **Can/May I?** Posso...? posso?

- ✪ **I would like...** Vorrei... vorrayee

HELPFUL PHRASES

- ✪ **Is this the way to...?** E'questa la strada per...? ay kwaystah lah strahdah payr...?

- ✪ **Could you point it out on the map?** Me lo può indicare sulla mappa? may lo pwo eendeekahray soollah mahppah?

- ✪ **Straight ahead** Diritto dreetto

- ✪ **Next to** Accanto a ahkkahnto ah

- ✪ **I'm in a hurry** Ho fretta o frayttah

- ✪ **Could you repeat that, please?** Potrebbe ripetermelo per favore? potraybbay reepayhtayrmaylo?

- ✪ **I don't understand** Non capisco non kahpeesko

- ✪ **Could you speak more slowly, please?** Potrebbe parlare un po' più lentamente? potraybbay pahrlahray oon po peeoo layntahmayntay?

- ✪ **Could you write it down?** Potrebbe

scrivermelo? potraybbay skreevayrmaylo?

- ✪ **Do you speak English?** Lei parla inglese? layee pahrlah eenglaysay?

- ✪ **I don't know** Non lo so non lo so

- ✪ **Can I smoke here?** Si può fumare qui? see pwo foomahray kwee?

- ✪ **Where can I find a taxi around here?** Dove posso prendere un taxi qui vicino? dovay posso prayndayray oon tahxee kwee veecheeno?

USEFUL WORDS AND PHRASES

NUMERALS

1	uno	oono
2	due	dooay
3	tre	tray
4	quattro	kwahttro
5	cinque	cheenkway
6	sei	sayèe
7	sette	sayttray
8	otto	otto
9	nove	novay
10	dieci	deeaychèe
11	undici	oondeechee
12	dodici	dodeechee
13	tredici	traydeechee
14	quattordici	kwahttordeechee
15	quindici	kweendeechee
16	sedici	saydeechee
17	diciassette	deechahssettay
18	diciotto	deecheeotto
19	diciannove	deechahnnovay
20	venti	vayntee
21	ventuno	vayntoono
22	ventidue	vaynteedoonay
30	trenta	trayntah
40	quaranta	kwahrahntah
50	cinquanta	cheekwahntah
60	sessanta	sayssahntah
70	settanta	sayttahntah
80	ottanta	ottahntah
90	novanta	novahntah
100	cento	chaynto
200	duecento	dooaychaynto
1000	mille	meelay
2000	duemila	dooaymeelah

GREETINGS

- **Good morning** Buon giorno *bwon jorno*
- **Good afternoon/evening** Buonasera *bwona sayrah*
- **Good night** Buona notte *bwonah nottay*
- **Hello/goodbye** Ciao *chow*
- **Yes/No** Si/No *see/no*
- **Please** Per Favore *pair fahvoaray*
- **Thank you (very much)** Mille grazie *meellay grahtzeeay*
- **You're welcome** Di niente/nulla *dee neeayntay/noollah*
- **How are you?** Come va? *komay vah?*
- **Very well, and you?** Benissimo, e lei? *bayneesseemo, ay layee?*
- **What is your name?** Come si chiama? *komay tee keeahmee?*
- **My name's ...** Mi chiamo.... *mee keeahmo...*
- **Delighted (to meet you)** Molto piacere (di conoscerla) *moalthoa peeahchayray*
- **This is my wife (husband)** Le/ti presento mia moglie/mio marito *lay/tee praysaynto meeah mollyay/meeo mahreeto*
- **See you later** A presto *ah praysto*
- **Have a good trip** Buon viaggio *bwon veeahdjo*
- **All the best** Tante belle cose *tahntay bayllay kozay*

DIFFICULTIES

- **Help!** Aiuto! *ayooto!*
- **Can you help me please?** Mi potrebbe aiutare? *mee oitraybbay aheeootahray?*
- **I'm sorry** Mi dispiace *mee deespeeahchay*
- **Excuse me...** Mi scusi... *mee skoozee*
- **Is there a toilet?** C'e un bagno? *cheh oon bahneeo*
- **Where is the telephone?** Dov'e il telefono? *doveh il taylayfono?*
- **Will you give me a telephone token, please?** Mi da un gettone, per favore? *mee dah oon jettone pair fahvoaray?*
- **What's the emergency number?** Qual è il numero dei servizi di emergenza? *kwahlay ay eel noomayro dayee sayrveetzee dee aymayrjayntzah?*
- **I've lost my wallet/purse** Ho perso il portafoglio/portamonete *o payrso eel portah-follyo/portahmonaytay*

USEFUL WORDS AND PHRASES

GOING SHOPPING

Is there a supermarket near here? C'èn un supermercato qui vicino? *chai oon soopair-mayrkartoa kooee veecheenoa?*

What time do the shops close? A che ora chiudono i negozi? *a ke ora kyoodono ee negotsi?*

What time do they open in the afternoon? A che ora aprono il pomeriggio? *a ke ora aprono il pomeereejo?*

Are they open on Sundays? Sono aperti la domenica? *sono apairti la domenica?*

Good morning. Can I help you? Buon giorno. Desidera? *bwon jorno. dezldera?*

This one/That one Questo/Quello *kwaysto/kwayllo*

I'll take this one Prendo questo/a qui *praundo kwaysto/ah kwee*

Could you slice it/cut it up? Me lo potrebbe affettare/tagliare a pezzi? *may lo potraybbay ahffayttahray/tahlllyahray ah paytzee?*

What's in it? Cosa c'è dentro? *kosah chay dayntro?*

How much does ... cost? Quanto costa ...? *kwanhnto costa?*

Is it fresh? E' fresco? *Eh fraysko?*

How much does ... weigh? Quanto pesa ...? *kwanhnto phsa?*

Here you are! Anything else? Tenga! Altro? *tenga altro?*

Yes, I'd also like... Si, mi dia anche... *see, mee deeah ahnkay...*

Where are the drinks? Dove sono le bevande? *doavay soanoa lay bayvahnday?*

Do you have cold beers? Avete delle birre fredde? *ahvaytay dayllay beerray fraydday?*

Where can I buy a can-opener? Dove posso comprare un apribot-tiglia? *doavay posssoa koampayrarray oon ahpreebottelyah?*

Without heads and filleted Sera testa e tagliato a filetti *sentsa taystah ay tahyartoa a feelayttoa*

No thank you, that's all No grazie, basta cosi *no grahtzeeay, bahstah cozee*

May I help/serve myself? Posso fare da me? *posso fahre da meh*

At the cash desk, please Alla cassa per favore. *alla cassa pair fahvoaray*

Thank you. Good day Grazie. Buon giorno. *gratsieh. bwon jorno*

MONEY

Where can I cash some traveller's cheques? Dove posso incassare questo traveller cheque? *dovay posso eenkahssahray kwaysyo trahvayllayr shayk?*

Can I pay by credit card? Potrei pagare con una carta di credito? *potrayee pahgahray kon oonah kahrtn dee kraydeeto?*

Where can I find a bank? Scusi, c'è una banca? *skoozee, chay oonah bahnnah?*

TIME

What's the time? Che ore sono? *kay oray sono?*

It's 6 o'clock Sono le sei. *sono lay sayèe*

Early, late Presto, tardi *praysto, tahrdee*

Tomorrow Domani *domahee*

Yesterday Ieri *eeayree*

WEIGHTS AND MEASURES

1 kg (kilo) Un chilo *oon keelo*

2 kg Due chili *dooe keeli*

100 g Cento grammi *chento grammi*/un etto *oon etto*

200 g (grams) Due etti *dooe etti*

500 g Mezzo chilo *meddzo keelo*

1 litre Un litro *oon leetro*

¾ trequarti *trequarti*

½ mezzo *meddzo*

¼ un quarto *un quarto*

a portion of una porzione di *oona portsione di*

½ portion of mezza porzione *meddza portsione di*

a glass of un bicchiere di *oon bickiere di*

a cup of una tazza di *oona tattsa di*

a slice of una fettina di *oona letteena di*

a piece of un pezzo di *con pettso di*

a fillet of un filetto di *oon filetto di*

USEFUL WORDS AND PHRASES

AT THE RESTAURANT

✪ **What time does the restaurant open?** A che ora apre il ristorante? *ah kay orah ahpray eel reestorahntay?*

✪ **Good evening, how many?** Buona sera, quante persone? *bwona sera, quante pairsone?*

✪ **Good morning, I'd like to book a table for four this evening** Buon giorno, vorrei prenotare un tavolo per quattro stasera *bwon jorno, vorrehi prenotare oon tahvolo pair kwahttro stasera*

✪ **Very well, what's your name?** Va bene, quale è il suo nome? *va bene, quahle eh il sooho nome?*

✪ **May we sit down?** Possiamo sederci? *possiamo sederchi?*

✪ **Have you any...please?** Avete del...per favore? *avete del ... pair favoaray?*

✪ **Could we see the menu?** Ci porta il menù *chee portah eel maynoo?*

✪ **What do you recommend?** Cosa ci consiglia? *kosah chee konseellyah?*

✪ **What's this?** Cosa è questo? *kosah ay kwaysto?*

✪ **This is not what I ordered** Non ho ordinato questo piatto *non o ordeenahto kwaysto peeahtto*

✪ **May I change my order?** Posso cambiare la mia ordinazione? *possoa kahmbeearray la meeah oardeenatseeoanee?*

✪ **Can we have some more bread?** Possoano avere un poco più di pane? *posssearmoa ahvayray oon pokoa peeoo dee parnay?*

✪ **We would like something to drink** Vorremmo ordinare qualcosa da bere *vorrehmmoa oardeenaray kwahilka-wsasah dali bayray*

✪ **A bottle of red wine** Una bottiglia di vino rosso *oonah botteelyah dee venoa rosssoa*

✪ **Can you recommend a local wine?** Può consigliare del vino della casa? *pwo konseellyahray dayl veenoa dellah karssah?*

✪ **We would like coffee** Vorremmo del caffè *vorrehmmoa dayl kahffay?*

✪ **Waiter, the bill please** Cameriere, Il conto per favore *kahmayreeayray ilo konto pair fahvoaray*

✪ **Keep the change** Tenga il resto *Tayngah eel raysto*

✪ **This is for you** Ecco a lei *aykkoh ah lay*

✪ **Could I have a receipt please?** Mi potrebbe dare una ricevuta per favore? *mee potraybbay dahray oonah reechayvootah pair fahvoaray?*

✪ **We didn't have this** Non abbiamo preso questo *non ahbbeeahmo prayso kwaysto*

✪ **Will you call the manager?** Mi chiama il capo-servizio? *mee keeahmah eel kahpo-sayrveetzeeo?*

SPECIAL REQUIREMENTS

✪ **For the baby (boy/girl)** Per il bambino/per la bambina *pair il bahmbeeno/pair la bahmbeenah*

✪ **Do you have a highchair (per bambini)?** Ha un seggiolone (per bambini)? *ah oon saydjolonay (payr bahmbeenee)?*

✪ **Could you warm up the baby's bottle?** Potrebbe riscaldare questo biberon? *potraybbay reeskahldahray kwaysyo beebayron?*

✪ **May I have a plate/spoon?** Posso avere un piatto/ cucchiaio? *possoa ahvayray oon peeahtto/ kookkeeaheeo?*

✪ **Could I have a glass of water?** Mi porta un bicchiere d'acqua? *me portah oon beekkeeayray dahkwah?*

✪ **Without dressing/oil** Senza condimento/olio *sentsa condimento/oleeo*

✪ **Does it have...in it?** Contiene...? *konteeayhnay...?*

✪ **I'm a vegetarian** Sono vegetariano *sono vayjaytahreeahno*

✪ **Is this sweet?** E'dolce? *ay dolchay?*

✪ **I'm on a salt-free diet** non posso mangiare sale *non posso mahnjahray sahlay*

✪ **Could I have the salt and pepper** Mi porta il sale e il pepe *mee portah eel sahlay ay eel paypay*

✪ **A half portion** Una mezza porzione *oona meddza portsione*

✪ **cold/hot** freddo/caldo *frayddo/kahldo*

✪ **raw/burnt** crudo/bruciato *kroodo/broochahto*

123

CONVERSION TABLES

NOTES ON USING THE RECIPES

Weights and measures are written in metric and imperial. Follow only one set of measure as they are not interchangeable.

ABBREVIATIONS

Metric	Imperial
g – gram or gramme	oz – ounce
kg – kilogram	lb – pound
ml – millilitre	fl oz – fluid oz

FLUID CONVERSIONS

125ml/4fl oz	500ml/18fl oz
150ml/¼ pint (5fl oz)	600ml/1 pint (20fl oz)
175ml/6fl oz	750ml/1¼ pints
200ml/7fl oz	1 litre/1¾ pints
300ml/½ pint (10fl oz)	2 litres/3½ pints

WEIGHT CONVERSIONS

50g/2oz	175g/7oz	700g/1½lb
75g/3oz	250g/9oz	1kg/2lb
100g/4oz	350g/12oz	1.5kg/3lb
150g/6oz	500g/1lb	2kg/4lb

SPOON MEASURES

Spoon measures refer to the standard measuring spoons and all quantities are level unless otherwise stated. Do not use table cutlery and serving spoons as their capacity varies.
½ teaspoon – 2.5ml
1 teaspoon – 5ml
1 tablespoon – 15ml (3 teaspoons)

OVEN TEMPERATURES

The following settings are used in the recipes in this book, providing centigrade, Fahrenheit and gas settings. However, cooking facilities in holiday accommodation may be limited or oven settings may be different or unreliable, therefore watch dishes carefully when baking in unfamiliar appliances.

110°C	225°F	gas ¼
120°C	250°F	gas ½
140°C	275°F	gas 1
150°C	300°F	gas 2
160°C	325°F	gas 3
180°C	350°F	gas 4
190°C	375°F	gas 5
200°C	400°F	gas 6
220°C	425°F	gas 7
230°C	450°F	gas 8
240°C	475°F	gas 9

AMERICAN MEASURES AND TERMS

Liquids:	Imperial	American
	5fl oz	⅔ cup
	8fl oz	1 cup
	10fl oz	1⅓ cups
	16fl oz	2 cups
	20fl oz (1 pint)	2½ cups

Solids: Whole pounds and fractions of a pound are used for some ingredients, such as butter, vegetables and meat. Cup measures are used for storecupboard foods, such as flour, sugar and rice. Butter is also measured by sticks.

	Imperial	American
Butter	8oz	1 cup (2 sticks)
Cheese, grated hard	4oz	1 cup
Flour	4oz	1 cup
Haricot beans, dried	6oz	1 cup
Mushrooms, sliced	8oz	2½ cups
Olives, whole	4oz	1 cup
Parmesan cheese, grated	1oz	3 tablespoons, 2oz/⅓ cup
Peas, shelled	4oz	1 cup
Raisins	6oz	1 cup
Rice (uncooked)	8oz	1 cup

Acknowledgements

The Automobile Association wishes to thanks the following photographers and libraries for their assistance in the preparation of this book.

ANTHONY BLAKE PHOTO LIBRARY F/C (d) (Graham Kirk), 34 (Gerrit Buntrock), 41 (Joff Lee), 49 (Amanda Heywood), 59 (Graham Kirk), 65 (Martin Brigdale), 69 (S. Lee Studios), 72 (Sian Irvine), 96 (Chris Bayley); GETTYONE/STONE 5b; ROBERT HARDING PICTURE LIBARY 37, 75b, 90, 92, 94, 97b, 100b; IMAGES COLOUR LIBRARY F/C (b); POWERSTOCK/ZEFA 95b; WORLD PICTURES 75a, 91b;

All remaining pictures are held in the Association's own library (AA PHOTO LIBRARY) with contributions from the following photographers:
P BENNETT 11b; J EDMANSON 53; J HOLMES 46; M JOURDAN 101c, 117b; E MEACHER 102b, 104b, 107b, 108b, 111b, 112b, 114b; K PATERSON 16/17, 27, 36, 38, 44, 52, 71, 76, 88; C SAWYER F/C (a), 2, 4, 5a, 7, 8, 9, 10a, 11a, 12a, 13a, 13b, 15, 18, 19a, 20a, 20b, 21a, 21b, 22a, 22b, 23a, 24a, 24b, 25, 30, 45, 50, 55, 56, 73, 86, 99, 101b, 117a; T SOUTER F/C (c), B/C, 1, 10b, 12b, 14, 19b, 23b, 28, 31, 33, 39, 43, 48, 58, 61, 62, 63, 66, 67, 70, 74, 77, 78, 79, 80, 81, 82, 83, 87, 89, 91a, 93, 95a; P WILSON 6, 97a, 98, 100a, 101a, 102a, 103, 104a, 105, 106, 107a, 108a, 109, 110, 111a, 112a, 113, 114a, 115, 116a, 116b

Written by: Susan Conte   Consultant: Bridget Jones   Managing Editor: Jackie Staddon

Dear Essential Traveller

Your comments, opinions and recommendations are very important to us. So please help us to improve our travel guides by taking a few minutes to complete this simple questionnaire.

You do not need a stamp (unless posted outside the UK). If you do not want to cut this page from your guide, then photocopy it or write your answers on a plain sheet of paper.

Send to: **The Editor, AA World Travel Guides, FREEPOST SCE 4598, Basingstoke RG21 4GY.**

Your recommendations...

We always encourage readers' recommendations for restaurants, nightlife or shopping – if your recommendation is used in the next edition of the guide, we will send you a **FREE** AA *Essential* **Guide** of your choice. Please state below the establishment name, location and your reasons for recommending it.

_____

_____

_____

_____

Please send me **AA *Essential*** _____

(*see list of titles inside the front cover*)

About this guide...

Which title did you buy?

AA *Essential* _____

Where did you buy it? _____

When? m̲ m̲ / y̲ y̲

Why did you choose an AA *Essential* Guide? _____

_____

_____

_____

_____

Did this guide meet your expectations?

Exceeded ☐   Met all ☐   Met most ☐   Fell below ☐

Please give your reasons _____

_____

_____

_____

continued on next page...

Were there any aspects of this guide that you particularly liked? _____

_____

_____

_____

Is there anything we could have done better? _____

_____

_____

_____

_____

About you…

Name (*Mr/Mrs/Ms*) _____

Address _____

_____

_____ Postcode _____

Daytime tel nos _____

Which age group are you in?
Under 25 ☐   25–34 ☐   35–44 ☐   45–54 ☐   55–64 ☐   65+ ☐

How many trips do you make a year?
Less than one ☐   One ☐   Two ☐   Three or more ☐

Are you an AA member? Yes ☐   No ☐

About your trip…

When did you book? m m / y y   When did you travel? m m / y y
How long did you stay? _____
Was it for business or leisure? _____
Did you buy any other travel guides for your trip?
    If yes, which ones? _____

_____

Thank you for taking the time to complete this questionnaire. Please send
    it to us as soon as possible, and remember, you do not need a stamp
    (*unless posted outside the UK*).

Happy Holidays!